What they're saying about
Actions against Distractions
by Geraldine Markel, PhD

This book can benefit everyone: professionals, business owners, artists, musicians, parents, and anyone trying to juggle a busy life. Dr. Markel's book is remarkable in that it helps you identify your own "Demons of Distraction" and, through reflection, mobilize yourself to overcome both internal and external interferences to achieving your goals. I found it funny, profoundly truthful, and enormously helpful.

SALLY ROSENBERG, MD
Associate Clinical Professor
Department of Psychiatry, Michigan State University

Actions against Distractions is a tremendously useful book aimed at enhancing our ability to transform intentions into productive actions. Readers discover a gold mine of practical applications, tips, and worksheets to make their lives better by getting more done in an organized manner.

FRANK PETROCK, PhD
President, General Systems Consulting Group, Inc.

We all struggle with distractions. If you want a breakthrough in productivity and staying laser-focused, distract yourself one last time and read this book. Talk is cheap. It's action that produces results, and Markel shows you how to internally master self-defeating patterns that stop you from reaching your goals. I highly recommend this tool.

SHAWNE DUPERON
Six-Time EMMY® Winner, ShawneTV

Dr. Markel's deep insights into the forces that distract us all continue in this new work that focuses the reader on how to turn good intentions into effective actions. The book is full of new ideas, practical tools, and coaching structures designed to help us overcome the overwhelm often caused by the distractions all around us.

DAVID CHINSKY, DrPH
Institute for Leadership Fitness
Author of *The Fit Leader's Companion*:
A Down-to-Earth Guide for Sustainable Leadership Success

Also by the Author

BOOKS

Defeating the 8 Demons of Distraction:
Proven Strategies to Increase Productivity and Decrease Stress

A Study Tip a Day Gets You an "A":
365 Secrets to Study Success

Finding Happiness with Aristotle as Your Guide:
Action Strategies Based on 10 Timeless Ideas (with Gary Madvin)

Finding Your Focus:
Practical Strategies for the Everyday Challenges Facing Adults with ADD
(with Judith Greenbaum, PhD)

Solving the College Admissions Puzzle:
A Guide for Students and Families About College Selection, Essay Writing, and
High-Stakes Testing
(with John B. Boshoven and Debbie E. Merion)

Helping Adolescents with ADHD and Learning Disabilities:
Ready-to-Use Tips, Techniques, and Checklists for School Success
(with Judith Greenbaum, PhD)

Performance Breakthroughs for Adolescents with Learning Disabilities or ADD:
How to Help Students Succeed in the Regular Education Classroom
(with Judith Greenbaum, PhD)

Peterson's Parent's Guide to the SAT and ACT:
Practical Advice to Help You and Your Teen
(with Linda Bizer, EdD)

Parents Are to Be Seen AND Heard:
Assertiveness in Educational Planning for Handicapped Children
(with Judith Greenbaum, PhD)

PRODUCTS

Defeating the Demons of Distraction
(Self-Coaching Card Deck)

Defeating the Demons of Distraction:
111 Ways to Improve Work/Life Performance and Decrease Stress
(Booklet)

ACTIONS Against Distractions:

Managing Your Scattered, Disorganized, and Forgetful Mind

Geraldine Markel, PhD

Author of *Defeating the 8 Demons of Distraction: Proven Strategies to Improve Productivity and Decrease Stress*

iUniverse LLC
Bloomington

ACTIONS AGAINST DISTRACTIONS:
MANAGING YOUR SCATTERED, DISORGANIZED, AND FORGETFUL MIND

iUniverse books may be ordered through booksellers or by contacting:

iUniverse
1663 Liberty Drive
Bloomington, IN 47403
www.iuniverse.com
1-800-Authors (1-800-288-4677)

Text illustrations: Chris Bidlack Creative Group, Ann Arbor, MI
Book Cover: Barbara Gunia, Sans Serif, Inc. Saline, MI

ISBN: 978-1-4759-9272-4 (sc)
ISBN: 978-1-4759-9273-1 (e)

Printed in the United States of America

iUniverse rev. date: 8/23/2013

Dedicated to my aunt, Roz Schwartz,
and my cousin, Mark Schwartz—
loved ones who were never distracted from
their devotion to family, friends, and community.

Contents

Acknowledgments

This book was completed with the help of a number of people. I am particularly grateful for the help received from those who took the time to read the first drafts of the manuscript and provided comments and insights about possible changes. Sheila Feigelson, PhD, spent numerous early-morning hours making notes and suggestions. Our conversations reflected her keen insights and sense of humor. Jane Heineken, Managing Your Mind associate and editor, provided invaluable ideas with respect to organization and flow. I'm especially indebted to the professional contribution of Barbara McNichol of Barbara McNichol Editorial. She provided the perfect blend of expertise, patience, and creativity. Always prompt and efficient, her attention to detail and clarity was a major contribution. For the illustrations of the demons, many thanks go to Chris Bidlack and staff of Bidlack Creative Group. Of course, special appreciation for the cover and interior design goes to Barbara Gunia and staff of Sans Serif, Inc., Saline, Michigan. Their creativity and expertise were especially important. Lastly, I am indebted to my husband, Shel, who provides constant support and inspiration.

The journey of a thousand miles
begins with one step.

—Chinese proverb

Preface

Confronted with today's uncertainties and challenges, how can you stop the distractions that impede your best intentions to be productive and feel peaceful?

Distractions deplete your psychic energy and divert your attention from important tasks, creating a barrier to being productive. Even before the emergence of Twitter, reports indicated that a worker's mind wanders for about one-third of the workday (Associated Press, 2007). Distractions also contribute to forgetfulness and disorganization.

When you're overwhelmed by distractions, perhaps you freeze in frustration and fail to act. Don't buy into that! You have the power to take the first step. This guide invites you to create a Plan of Attack against the distractions that thwart your efforts to enjoy your work/life endeavors.

As an educational psychologist and coach, I assist individuals, leaders, and teams in performing better and faster, with less stress—at work, in school, or at home. When I need to stay on track, increase my productivity, or decrease stress, I rely on the same simple yet powerful strategies that I teach. They have grown out of decades of research on learning, performance, and cognitive behavioral therapy. I adapt the research to the tasks at hand and my personal style.

Why turn to research? Isn't dealing with distractions a matter of self-discipline?

Here's the problem: Your intelligence and intuition are not enough to achieve sustained behavior change. Making necessary changes requires a combination of smarts, motivation, strategy, and support—especially when dealing with the myriad distractions in today's frenetic, multitasking culture. Because of competing values, demands, and consequences, it's common to lack the motivation to start—and stick to—a viable plan for increasing productivity.

Yes, to become more efficient requires a Plan of Attack for altering your patterns. That means learning new strategies and setting up new routines. Although that's always been difficult, it's even trickier when life has you constantly "running for the next train."

In *Defeating the 8 Demons of Distraction: Proven Strategies to Increase Productivity and Decrease Stress*, I answered such questions as, "What are the most common kinds of distractions?" and "How do the destructive forces of distraction interfere with work/life productivity and satisfaction?" I used the term *demon* to amuse, but it also emphasizes the negative forces that contribute to instability and waste—especially the waste of time, money, and motivation. When demons are pervasive, it might feel futile to even attempt making a meaningful change. That book stresses awareness, insight, and basic aids.

However, awareness and basic tools simply aren't enough to create long-term change. That's why I wrote this step-by-step action guide. It coaches you to align proven strategies with your unique strengths, vulnerabilities, interests, and style, addig up to real change.

The purpose of this book is to help you move from good intentions to productive action. As you dig in, you'll see that *Actions Against Distractions: Managing Your Scattered, Disorganized, and Forgetful Mind* can help you:

- Discover your distraction-related strengths and vulnerabilities

- Inspire your transition from good intentions to effective action

- Gain and maintain improved attention, memory, and organization

- Enjoy greater peace of mind and life satisfaction

Use *Actions Against Distractions* separately or in tandem with *Defeating the 8 Demons of Distraction* to effect the changes you want—and enjoy living your life well!

Introduction

The New York Times headline read, PRESIDENT OF TOKYO STOCK EXCHANGE RESIGNS. The cause? This executive assumed responsibility for a computer error that contributed to a $350 million trading loss and raised doubts about the exchange's ability to handle increasingly heavy volume. This error and resulting upheaval at the world's second largest stock exchange was due to a brokerage firm's employee error during the preholiday season. He had mistyped a sale order, flooding the market with 610,000 shares of stock at one yen per share, worth less than a penny each. He was supposed to sell only one share at 610,000 yen, priced at $5,200 in US dollars (Flacker, 2005).

This trading mishap provides a glaring example of how technology glitches and human error can have terrifying effects on us—individually, nationally, and internationally. A split second of distraction can result in huge losses.

Not all distractions lead to horrific consequences, but they do lead to frustration and stress. What about you? Does it seem like mysterious forces are engulfing you and thwarting your efforts to be efficient? How many times have you said, "I wish I weren't constantly being interrupted all day," or "I need to stop wasting time on the computer," or "I'm running from one thing to another, and I feel like I never get anything done"?

Take Cover! The Demons of Distraction Attack

How much time, money, or turmoil does distraction cost you? Have you ever:

- Missed a deadline at work and couldn't make up for it?

- Replaced lost checks, receipts, or theater tickets?

- Lost or sat on expensive glasses and had to buy new ones?

- Glanced away and dented your car door or fender, incurring hundreds of dollars in repair costs?

- Paid late-payment penalties for bills or taxes?

Consider how much more money could be in your pocket if you'd paid better attention to detail. Yes, it's time to stop these costly distractions. But how?

Face the Issue Straight On

First, although you might prefer to minimize or dismiss the effects of distraction, consider facing the issue straight on instead. Analyze the often irritating and sometimes disastrous effects of distractions on your work/life. Witness how toxic their power becomes when the demons join forces. And ask, "To what degree does my fast-track life create a playground for the Demons of Distraction? Are any of these demons fostering flaky, forgetful, disorganized behavior—and increasing my stress?"

Understand that there's an inverse relationship between a distraction and the effectiveness of your attention, memory, organization, and motivation. For example, the more stress or interruptions, the less mental energy you have for focusing.

Second, create a Plan of Attack—a systematic approach that fits your talents and vulnerabilities. Decide how to attack and rid your work/life of needless distractions. Use the system in these twelve chapters to help you develop your own Plan of Attack and implement and obtain support for it. You'll discover how to conquer the eight most common Demons of Distraction. Although each demon is discussed separately, in reality, they often attack together, and the damage they cause spirals out of control. For example, frequent interruptions result in uneven work patterns. Then you push hard to catch up, expend more energy, and experience greater stress. Often, sleeping problems follow. With fatigue comes frustration and perhaps headaches. You slow down—and so does your productivity. The more your ability to be productive deteriorates, the more overwhelmed, forgetful, and disorganized you become. Before long, you're sliding down the slippery slope to failure. Face that possibility straight on, and allow each chapter to spur you to action. You'll be amazed at how fast you can progress.

What can you expect to discover in the next twelve chapters?

- Stories and statistics to arouse your interest in specific distractions

- Self-checks and questions to increase your awareness about the degree to which you may be impeded by these Demons of Distraction

- Charts and checklists to deepen your mindfulness about the frequency and the conditions under which you experience various distractions

- Research-based strategies to adapt and improve your work/life productivity

- Special issues and barriers that appear when you attempt to move from intention to action

- Contracts and action plans to facilitate planning, monitoring, and maintaining progress

You'll find the systematic approach in this book especially helpful if you currently:

- Struggle to maintain your job or find a new one

- Have to come out of retirement to pay your bills

- Need to find the time and energy to go to school or change careers

- Deal with constant changes in technology and job requirements

- Strive to improve so you can keep ahead of your competitors

- Fight a losing battle with fatigue, rushing, and overcommitment

- Desire improvement in your ability to remember and organize details

Adopt the ideas in this book in ways that seem right for you, either in the order presented or starting with the problem that interests you most. Keep in mind that when facing your demons, adopting a simple, flexible approach fosters the most rapid improvement.

It's time to marshal your forces and start stamping out the Demons of Distraction that hinder your efforts too often. Onward!

Your Demons of Distraction

Bill and his officemates are engaged in teasing banter and hearty laughter over drinks and dinner. The egg rolls and fried wontons taste delicious, despite being rather greasy. Reveling in food, friends, and fun, Bill grabs a cloth napkin and wipes his mouth with gusto. When his friends suddenly whoop and point, he realizes that he's used his new designer silk tie as his napkin. Oops!

Does this story represent a silly incident or a more serious problem? Bill's expensive cleaning bills attest to his frequent carelessness at social occasions. How much do distractions like this foster a messy work style and tarnish Bill's professional image—which could cost him dearly?

How about you? Have you been embarrassed by similar performance slippages? If you experience work/life distractions that diminish your best efforts, it's time to pay attention. You don't want occasional incidents to develop into nasty habits that pose significant barriers to attaining your work/life goals.

It's time to ask these questions:

- Am I suffering constant and irritating distractions?

- To what degree do distractions lead to inattention, forgetfulness, and disorganization?

- What are the costs and consequences of distractions at work or home?

- How do distractions undermine my attempts to live a life aligned with my deepest values?

This chapter addresses these questions and provides self-checks, activities, and daily logs to identify your demons and their costs and to set preliminary goals.

Define the Consequences of Your Distraction

Charlie Ponte, my dad, built a musical instrument business in midtown Manhattan. On one hand, he loved selling, and he enjoyed the camaraderie of other musicians. On the other hand, he was inattentive to management responsibilities like signing insurance policies and leases. When the Rockefellers bought the block of buildings on Forty-Eighth Street, all the storeowners who had signed their leases received a million dollars to vacate. Because Mr. Ponte hadn't signed his lease, not only did he not get a million dollars, he suffered a lawsuit because he didn't vacate before the Christmas season sales.

Like Charlie Ponte, many Americans don't complete their important financial responsibilities. For example, putting off filing their taxes costs Americans a collective $400 million dollars a year in penalties (Steele, 2007).

Financial consequences can be critical but aren't fatal. Yet many stories in the news report the serious and even deadly results of inattention and distraction. For example, pilots' social interaction and inattention appear to contribute to plane crashes (Kavanagh, 2009). Add that to reports about drivers killing themselves (and others) due to distractions like texting or cell phone use while driving.

Wherever inattention and distraction occur, their consequences warrant your immediate review. In the chart that follows, check any of the items that apply to you. Be sure to jot down any other consequences that apply.

Self-Check: Negative Consequences of Distractions

Work Life

____ Performance. Allowing performance to falter due to forgetfulness or overlooked details

____ Organization. Losing and misplacing papers or dealing with constant clutter

____ Planning. Responding reactively rather than proactively to opportunities or problems

___ Communication. Neglecting team or supervisor responsibilities, providing incomplete directions, frequently changing your mind or second-guessing others

___ Career Path. Struggling on a slow career track or moving from job to job

___ Other. _____

Personal Life

___ Finance. Incurring unnecessary finance charges, losing invoices, misplacing tax receipts, or overspending

___ Time Management. Arriving late for meetings, procrastinating, or taking too long to complete chores

___ Health. Postponing medical and dental checkups, arriving late or missing appointments, or forgetting to comply with medical routines

___ Legal. Ignoring requests for information from tax or insurance agencies, losing or not paying traffic tickets, or not signing important papers, such as wills, taxes, or leases

___ Stress. Lacking awareness of your emotional needs and vulnerabilities or succumbing to needless irritability, frustration, or stress

___ Home Maintenance. Neglecting the upkeep of your car, home, or personal items or allowing excessive clutter in your closets, attic, garage, and/or basement

___ Other. _____

Social Life

___ Personal Relationships. Lacking sensitivity to social cues and not adjusting your behavior; lacking sensitivity about when to stop teasing or when to be empathetic

___ Communication. Being inattentive when listening and lax about keeping in touch with others; forgetting to reply to phone calls, correspondence, invitations, or e-mail

___ Commitment. Failing to follow through on obligations and promises, despite your good intentions

___ Stability. Behaving in an absentminded, inconsistent, or unpredictable way due to a loss of focus on your cherished values or goals

___ Responsibility and Respect. Lapsing into disorganization or messiness without regard to its effect on others

___ Other: _____

When you identify your own negative consequences, you increase the likelihood that you'll commit to setting goals and sticking to a plan. To reinforce what you've noticed, play a video in your mind about the role that distraction has played in your life/work in the last few months. Then, for each, briefly list the negative consequences you've experienced.

- Work Life _____

- Personal Life _____

- Social Life _____

Next, ask and answer these core questions:

- Am I suffering constant, irritating distractions?

- To what degree do distractions lead to inattention, forgetfulness, and disorganization?

- What are the costs and consequences of distractions at work or home?

- How do distractions undermine my attempts to live a life that is aligned with my deepest values?

What Positive Outcomes Do You Seek?

Jolie, a personal trainer, has identified situations that need her attention. Specifically, she gets distracted while talking to service personnel at banks, restaurants, and stores. During business transactions, she loses receipts and wastes time balancing her accounts. Consequently, she fails to collect the reimbursements to which she is entitled. Under Professional Life, she wrote the following goal: "More consistency when doing business activities, especially when storing receipts. Take fifteen seconds to put the receipts in my wallet as soon as they are received."

Follow Jolie's lead. Once you've identified problems and decided to make changes, take these steps:

1. Determine and list the overall positive outcomes you desire.

2. Mull over the items you've checked under each category.

3. Choose goals that will enhance work/life performance, boost profits, and increase your level of satisfaction.

It's easy to identify lots of areas, but start small and be specific. Select no more than two items from the following list. For example, if you seek greater accuracy in your performance at work or home, jot down something like, "Improve addition and completion on check registry and deposit slips."

Performance at work or home:

___ Greater accuracy

___ More consistency

___ Better organization

___ Improved attention and memory

___ Other: _____

Profitability:

___ Greater productivity

___ Greater financial gain

___ Greater security

___ Other: _____

Peacefulness at work or home:

___ Less frustration

___ Less stress

___ More motivation

___ More fun

___ Other: _____

The 8 Demons of Distraction

When you feel lazy, crazy, or dumb, it probably means you've encountered a Demon of Distraction. These demons come in a variety of forms. In sometimes insidious ways, one or more demons strike. The result? They wreak havoc on your performance, productivity, and peacefulness. "Know thy enemy" and prepare, so you can avoid the worst of their damage.

All eight Demons of Distraction are summarized here (Markel, 2008). An illustration of each demon is featured at the beginning of chapters three through ten.

- **The Technology Demon** prowls day and night. It invites you to get lost in a maze of texting, chatting, surfing, and gaming long after the time spent is appropriate or useful.

- **The *Others* Demon** has many faces: coworkers, bosses, significant others, and/ or children who believe you should be available twenty-four/seven. When you can't stop interruptions, set boundaries, or say no, you lose numerous opportunities for creativity.

- **The Activities Demon** attacks when you inappropriately multitask, travel, rush, or face tedious, difficult tasks. You're easy prey for distractions during emotional events, such as holidays and family gatherings.

- **The Spaces Demon** lurks where you live, work, or play. Distracted by sights and sounds or wallowing in messy, unpleasant settings, you are prone to feeling overwhelmed, producing inaccurate work, and working at a slow pace.

- **The Stress Demon** robs you of the psychic energy you need to pay attention.

Internal or external triggers, or a combination of both, activates this demon. Without conscious attention to your stress levels, you can make many mistakes and poor choices.

- **The Fatigue Demon** saps the energy you need to focus and maintain concentration. Although you try to deny it, feeling exhausted leaves you spinning your wheels, committing errors, or even causing accidents.

- **The Illness/Medication Demon** robs you of your vigor and can lead to emotional ups and downs. Your performance can plummet due to poor concentration, memory loss, confusion, insomnia, nausea, or headaches (often side effects of medication).

- **The Unruly-Mind Demon** can have three heads: hyper-focus, racing thoughts, or daydreaming. The more unruly your mind, the less productive you are.

Self-Check: My Demons of Distraction

Directions: Read each statement and check all that apply to you.

____ 1. I text, tweet, play games, or check sport or financial statistics excessively. (Technology Demon)

____ 2. I have a hard time saying no, I'm overcommitted, and I'm interrupted all day. (*Others* Demon)

____ 3. I feel pressure to multitask, but it doesn't work for me. (Activities Demon)

____ 4. My workspace is so noisy that I have trouble thinking. (Spaces Demon)

____ 5. I lack specific strategies to manage stress, so when I begin to work, I ruminate about problems and pressures. (Stress Demon)

____ 6. I'm frequently tired and find it hard to focus. (Fatigue Demon)

____ 7. I take medications that interfere with my attention and/or memory. (Medication/Illness Demon)

____ 8. Once I start to concentrate, I get lost in the task, and ignore everything— even when I'm not achieving much. (Unruly-Mind Demon: Hyper-focus)

___ 9. I try to finish tasks or chores but frequently find myself daydreaming. (Unruly Mind: Daydreaming)

___ 10. My mind races, and I can't seem to focus on one thing at a time. (Unruly Mind: Racing thoughts)

Assess: Current Distraction Attacks

A distraction attack is a momentary slippage of focus, often producing an amusing, inconsequential result. Perhaps you're aware that technology or other people can mess up your ability to concentrate. For example, you're holding a hardboiled egg in one hand and a cell phone in the other. The phone rings. You smack the egg into your ear!

What about factors like fatigue or stress? Dig deep to identify demons like this that may be interfering with your performance or peace of mind. To do so, visualize what happened during the past few days and list the peskiest demons you experienced. For each one, describe where you were, what the result was, and how you felt.

- Demon: _____

- Demon: _____

- Demon: _____

More often than you'd like, demons attack en masse. For example, when you feel tired and under pressure, you're more vulnerable to distraction from the Fatigue and Stress Demons. You might be especially vulnerable to the *Others* Demon, which shows up when you fly off the handle rather than ignore your coworker's interruption. Think about your current work/life situations and describe your most lethal combination of demons:

- Combination 1:_____

  _____

- Combination 2: _____

  _____

Once you identify your demons, explore ways these demons can influence your work/life.

Assess the Past: Successful and Unsuccessful Experiences

Can you remember life experiences when you dealt both successfully and unsuccessfully with distractions? By visualizing those occasions, you can more clearly identify what you did or didn't do to thwart distractions so they won't interfere with your actions again. When you write about previous experiences, you shed light on long-standing tendencies. Usually, it's more motivating to start with the successful experiences.

Your definition of success in doing this varies based on your interests and talents. For example, success is viewed different for a CEO or teacher. Here's an example of one describing a jazz singer/songwriter:

> *How could a beginning songwriter beat a racing mind, attain focus, and retain memory of her ideas and melodies? In the past, her thoughts about new songs would disappear faster than her glasses or keys. Now she records her creative ideas on her cell phone. Since setting this up, the number of songs she's created has increased significantly.*

This aspiring musician defines success as finding an aid against distraction. An accountant, on the other hand, might define success as getting away from office distractions by going to a library to complete an annual report.

The songwriter, like many people, likes to talk about her experiences. Others prefer to write about their experiences in a journal; still others choose to use a chart to organize their thoughts. For example, suppose the songwriter jotted notes on a chart about the lessons she learned. It would look like this:

The Songwriter's Successful Experience

Time of Life	Which Demon Did I Defeat?	What Was the Situation?	What Were the Consequences?	What Strategy Was Used?	What Lesson(s) Did I Learn?
Adult/ Work Life	Unruly Mind: Racing thoughts	I'd think of a great lyric but not stop to write it and then go on to the next idea.	I lost the thought and wasn't as productive as I could be.	Used a cell phone to record ideas as they raced through my mind. I enjoyed five times the productivity as before.	An aid is not a crutch. I need to capture my thoughts before I forget them.

To use a chart like this productively, remember or visualize times when you successfully warded off distractions, and then answer the questions. No need to include all the stages of your life; select the most memorable ones. After writing about a successful experience on the chart, you'll tackle an unsuccessful one next.

My Successful Experience

Time of Life	Which Demon Did I Defeat?	What Was the Situation?	What Were the Consequences?	What Strategy Was Used?	What Lesson(s) Did I Learn?
Elementary School					
Secondary School					
Postsecondary School					
First Years of Work					
Other					

The goal is to gain an historical perspective. Look for the positive patterns you used over time to avoid or defeat distractions. Then you can remember and repeat them.

Once you're aware of your successful distraction-defeating experiences, consider your less successful experiences and look for patterns in them. For example, Roger jotted down notes in chart form because for him, that was quick and easy. Roger's unsuccessful experience shows the disruption caused by a combined attack of the Activities and the Stress Demons before his vacation.

Roger's Unsuccessful Experience

Time of Life	Which Demon(s) Attacked?	What Was the Situation?	What Were the Consequences?	What Strategy Did I Use?	What Lesson(s) Did I Learn?
Adult/ Work Life	Stress and Activity Demons	Before leaving town, I ran around the house looking for the ticket, not knowing I'd left the butter on the table and put the tickets in the refrigerator.	Stressed out, I yelled about how we might miss our flight. My actions aggravated everyone in the family.	Put ticket and other travel documents by the door the night before departure.	Think and plan ahead. Make a list, check it twice, and organize early.

Remember or visualize times in your life when you didn't successfully ward off distractions; write them in the following chart. Jog your memory by addressing such questions as:

- What mistakes have occurred due to distractions during travel or while rushing?

- What frustrating experience could have been avoided if I was paying more careful attention to what I was doing?

My Unsuccessful Experiences

Time of Life	Which Demon Attacked?	What Was the Situation?	What Were the Consequences?	What Strategy Did I Use?	What Lesson(s) Did I Learn?
Elementary School					
Secondary School					
Postsecondary School					
First Years of Work					
Other					

Review your successful and unsuccessful past distraction-related experiences, and identify patterns or trends. Take the time to discuss your insights with others. Consider addressing such questions as:

- What patterns emerge?

- Where and when have I been most vulnerable to distractions?

- When and where have I been most successful in my attempts to reduce distractions?

- How do distractions undermine my attempts to live a life aligned with my deepest values?

Assess the Present: Keep a Distraction Attack Log

Keep a log of the demons that attack you. For at least three days, preferably longer, record the specifics: where, when, and for how long each distraction attack lasts. Describe how you felt during and after such attacks, and list consequences of the distraction attacks.

Distraction Attack Log

Which Demon(s)?	What Was the Situation?	What Were the Consequences?	What Strategy Did I Use?	What Lesson(s) Did I Learn?
1				
2				
3				
4				

Please don't be at the mercy of various distractions all day long. Ask:

* What is my distraction potential?

* How much time could I save each day or week if I experienced fewer distractions and interruptions?

* What is my current reality?

* What are my barriers to being more productive?

When you're sensitive to the ways distraction interferes with your work output (including your memory and organization), you naturally feel less stressed.

When the Demons Gang Up

Results can be devastating when several Demons of Distraction attack at the same time. With the onslaught of multiple demons, the flow of your work gets interrupted or stops altogether, creating debilitating cycles.

For example, if you have unclear directions or unrealistically high expectations about the task to be done, a debilitating cycle may begin as you start the activity. These thoughts distract you from the task. You wonder if you have the ability to do the job or meet the expectations; you feel overwhelmed. Your stress level increases, and your attention, motivation, and analytic thinking decrease. In fact, they can stall or stop completely.

At times, your racing mind yields a flood of ideas, and you can't make a decision about how to start. At other times, you hyper-focus on one unnecessary aspect you could do easily. You might work on a task or worry about an issue until exhaustion overwhelms you. When this occurs, your workflow is uneven or completely shuts down. The Unruly-Mind Demon undermines the Activities Demon and colludes with the Stress and Fatigue Demons. With these demons on the rampage, you experience "analysis paralysis."

Once you're aware of the nasty consequences imposed by simultaneous or cyclical attacks, you have a better chance of avoiding situations that create them. You identify pitfalls, pinpoint the circumstances to deal with first, and use your logical mind to lead the way to greater productivity. All this reduces your stress.

Distraction and Attention Deficit Disorder

It seems that everyone you meet alludes with humor to the idea that he or she suffers from Attention Deficit Disorder (ADD). Experiencing an occasional symptom, such as distractibility, isn't the same as having a disorder. A disorder or disability exists when a cluster of symptoms is pervasive and chronic. Functionally, the symptoms present significant barriers to one's performance and social relationships at work, school, and home (Barkley and Benton, 2010; Ramsey and Rostain, 2008; Brown, 2005; Barkley, 2005; Hallowell and Ratey, 2006; Markel and Greenbaum, 2005; Solden, 2002).

The term *Attention Deficit Disorder* applies to a person who experiences distractibility in addition to a short attention span, a tendency to disorganization, and a variety of other dysfunctions, including inability to manage time, organize, or plan. The term Executive Function Impairment may be used (Brown, 2008). When an individual experiences impulsivity and excess body movements, the term *Attention Deficit Hyperactivity Disorder* (ADHD) is applied. Many bright, competent individuals suffer from these symptoms but compensate for them—that is, until their lives become too complicated. ADD-related symptoms may eventually block them from fully expressing their potential. Thomas E. Brown, PhD, dispelled certain myths attached to ADD; he writes, "ADD is a chemical problem that undermines the management of systems of the brain, not just a lack of willpower" (Brown, 2005).

Based on studies by the Centers for Disease Control, it's estimated that 3 to 5 percent of the school-age population has ADD; some studies estimate up to 9 or 10 percent (CDDC, 2005). Among the adult population in the United States, an estimated 4 percent—eight million people—have this disability. Commonly, a person with ADD has other difficulties that are byproducts of ADD or coexist with ADD. For example, it's estimated that of those who have ADD, between 30 and 60 percent have a learning disability. In addition, significant numbers of those with ADD or ADHD experience depression and/or anxiety (Barkley, 2010). For anyone, emotional problems such as depression and anxiety can have disastrous effects on focus, concentration, motivation, and memory.

Most people who experience distraction, forgetfulness, and disorganization can look to our distraction-driven society as a factor. However, if you have more than a few of the above symptoms that lead to serious consequences—poor performance evaluation, poor academic performance, poor social relationships, even job loss—contact your physician or a psychologist for a neuropsychological evaluation. Also refer to books in the Resources section that address ADD so you can understand what your symptoms might mean (Sarris, 2011; Jacobs and Wendel, 2010; Tuckman, 2009).

Understand that you don't have to have ADD or ADHD to be distracted. Most people who experience distraction, forgetfulness, and disorganization are battling some *bad habits* within our distraction-driven society. Read on so you can create a Plan of Attack and take action against your Demons of Distraction.

Your 5-Step Plan of Attack

It's the day of the big birthday party. Peter is plowing through old photo albums to create a collage of his wife's best moments. He and his friend laugh and joke about their years of friendship and fun. They have a drink and finish up. Two hours later, Peter panics because he can't find the pack of photos. They're not underneath the couch or in the albums. He searches while his friend teases him. Chagrined and irritated at his poor memory and disorganization, he posts a single photo, his wife's baby picture, in the entrance hall and sighs, "I must be losing it."

A variety of negative effects relate to distractibility, including inattention and memory slippage. Some are obvious, others more subtle. For example, you may blame your memory for misplacing your keys or eyeglasses, but more likely, it's a problem involving your attention. Like Peter's lost photos, your ability to recall a piece of information can be thwarted because of inattention. A distraction, such as talking, drinking, or laughing, while you perform a task doesn't allow the information to be stored in your short-term memory. The myth of multitasking is discussed in chapter 6, "Actions Against the Activities Demon."

When you increase your use of proven, self-regulatory techniques, you'll have an easier time making a commitment to change—and dealing with distractions head-on. Adopt a systematic process and you'll have the tactics you need to confront and defeat your personal demons.

In addition to self-checks, this chapter gives you information about executive functioning, learning style, and attention triggers through five research-based action steps. The result? You'll create a Plan of Attack to curtail the disastrous effects of distraction on your work/life productivity.

Executive Functioning

Did you know that to activate and manage attention, you have to rely on a broad set of thinking functions? Just as a general presides over a command center, you have areas within your brain where you exert control over thinking, attention, and planning. These and other mental processes are labeled *executive functioning*. Like the conductor of an orchestra, the *executive* within our brain allows us to effectively plan, organize, strategize, pay attention, remember facts and details, and manage time and space.

Researchers indicate that attention is not a single, isolated act (Brown, 2008). Rather, it includes these functions:

- Activating attention: factors that arouse or trigger your attention

- Sustaining attention: factors that contribute to persistence while doing a task

- Switching focus from one thing to another: factors that allow you to balance attention between topics or tasks

- Screening out irrelevant stimuli: factors that help you ignore possible distractions or interruptions

Individuals vary in their capacities to access one or another aspect of attention. For example, you might put off beginning a task, but once you're involved, you sustain attention until you've completed it. Someone else might promptly start a task but be unable to keep doing it or, when necessary, switch from task to task. Still others may suffer from overload, become mentally paralyzed, and shut down altogether.

Attention Patterns

Once you understand aspects of attention, it's helpful to increase awareness of your particular attention patterns. For many, attention shifts according to their energy cycle. For instance, some people enjoy high energy and alertness in the morning, while for others attention peaks in the evening. You might experience high attention energy in a particular location, when working with others, or when you are relaxed. To be most productive, be aware of the times and conditions when you enjoy periods of peak attention and then schedule your tasks accordingly.

For example, Traci is a supervisor and technical writer. For a week, she noted the time frames, conditions, and attention peaks she experienced so she can work efficiently.

Traci realized that her most productive work occurs when she rises early and revs up before everyone else streams into the building. She's least able to concentrate when she's tired, stressed, feeling inadequate, or surrounded by others. Also, she realized that she is least attentive and most vulnerable to distraction when she tried to work at the end of the day when everyone was hanging around her office to chat.

It's your turn. Visualize events in your work/life during the last week. Use the following chart to note the times, tasks, and conditions when you attempted to be productive. If you want, rate the quality of your attention using a scale from one to ten, ten indicating the times you felt highly focused and productive.

My Times, Conditions, and Attention Peaks

	Sunday	Monday	Tuesday	Wednesday	Thursday	Friday	Saturday
Morning							
Afternoon							
Evening							

Your notes (or ratings) show that when you pay attention to *how you pay attention*, you:

- Gain insight about situations and conditions in which you pay attention most effectively

- Schedule times and establish conditions to complete your most important tasks quickly and accurately

- Feel confident about your ability to make profound improvements in your work/life.

Learning Styles

People differ in the ways they learn best (Gardner, 2006). Many people absorb information most easily when they use their hands and move around. They are body smart and comprehend best (and are distracted least) when they stand or walk as they memorize facts. Others are image smart. Show them an illustration and they remember it forever. Sometimes, people use several ways of learning information.

Monique, a graduate student in engineering, says her most effective manner of learning is to listen and write down information. She relies on listening, writing (tactile), and visual learning avenues. When listening, she is able to pay attention most effectively. She augments her learning by creating flash cards and diagrams.

Like most people, you probably have one or two "best" ways of learning. Your learning style indicates your most effective approach to paying attention. When you pay attention, the more reliance you place on your learning strength, the better you maintain your focus and keep distractions at bay.

What are your learning style strengths? Answer the following brief self-check to identify them. Read the statements listed below, and check all that reflect your preferred way of learning.

Self-Check: Ways I Learn Best

____ 1. I frequently need a diagram or illustration to understand or remember. (Visual)

____ 2. I would rather listen to a lecture than read a book. (Auditory)

____ 3. I'm good at putting things together, like puzzles. (Mechanical)

___ 4. I learn by participating in an activity or seeing a demonstration. (Kinesthetic/Hands-On)

___ 5. I learn best with stories and analogies. (Verbal)

___ 6. I frequently use musical jingles to learn things. (Musical)

___ 7. I'm a number person. I find it easy to use a formula. (Mathematical)

___ 8. I learn best when interacting with others. (Social)

The one or more items you checked tell you that when using those senses or modalities you're most alert and ready to receive information. To follow up, visualize some work or school experiences. Jot down your most and least effective ways of learning or retaining information here.

Most effective ways of learning: _____

Least effective ways of learning: _____

Learning Styles and Related Attention Triggers

Certain learning strengths involve specific triggers that easily activate your attention and learning. By using these triggers, you can better manage your actions, tasks, and work/life settings. Here are a few guidelines:

- If you learn best with visual aids, then write triggers on Post-it notes of various sizes and colors. Highlight directions with a colored marker. Use an automatic lighting device like a timed lamp to provide a signal for starting or stopping your activity.

- If you learn best when you hear information, then use sound devices, such as alarms, music, bells, and beepers, to trigger your attention. Most likely, you enjoy hearing stories and humor.

- If you learn best with numbers, then use numbered lists or geometric shapes as triggers. For example, the shape of a stop sign might signal you to stop to collect your papers before leaving the house.

- If you're a hands-on, or kinesthetic, person, then use a watch or mobile phone that vibrates to grab your attention.

- If you're a gregarious person, then you might focus most easily when interacting with others, especially when the task is boring or tedious. In such cases, you might use questions to evoke deeper thoughts and rely on verbal cues to maintain concentration.

The next part is to deploy your strengths in order to work around your vulnerabilities. This means being both grateful for your strengths and accepting of your vulnerabilities. Don't let pride prevent you from using special strategies to manage your vulnerabilities. For example, if you have difficulty remembering directions, don't fight it; just admit it. You know how to compensate: use a map, GPS, or service like MapQuest. If you have a problem listening to and remembering numbers, carry paper and pencil to jot down phone numbers and directions.

Whatever you do, don't berate yourself and think, *I'm just dumb. I should be able to do this.* If you feel embarrassed about using a tactic, prepare a face-saving statement, such as, "Give me a minute to jot this down—it's important to get it right." And relax!

Your 5-Step "Actions Against Distractions" Plan of Attack

Once you have noted your strengths and vulnerabilities in paying attention and determined your learning style, start fighting these "enemies" of executive function: distraction, interruption, and information overload. They're not only irritating; they reduce your attention, memory, and organizational skills. As a result, they also set the stage for a downward spiral of performance.

Yes, the Demons of Distraction exist within and around you, so, like a military strategist, create your Plan of Attack. That means identifying the "enemy"—where and when the most damage occurs—and systematically developing a plan that has the greatest chance of success.

Research on learning and behavior change indicates that a successful strategy includes a variety of elements (Rothwell et al., 2007; Rummler and Brache, 1995). The following steps will help you to develop a workable "Actions Against Distractions" Plan of Attack.

1. Assess level of distraction and productivity.

2. Analyze consequences.

3. Set realistic goals.

4. Take action.

5. Monitor, recognize, and maintain progress.

1. Assess Level of Distraction and Productivity

First, scratch the surface by completing the brief awareness checklist at the beginning of each chapter. This pinpoints ways distractions negatively affect your work/life productivity. Then pose questions about your distraction triggers, the length of time the interruptions last, and the degree to which they interfere with memory and organization.

When you write in a journal for a few minutes several times a week, you can easily and specifically assess your attention patterns, strengths, and vulnerabilities. What happens next? The assessment helps you clarify your jumbled thoughts and relieve tension. It also lets you view distraction as a problem to solve rather than something that spirals out of control.

Your journaling doesn't have to be "pretty" or belabored. Even index cards or dated scraps of paper tossed into a container can be used to record events or emotions. Later, you'll review these tidbits of information to identify patterns and provide insights.

2. Analyze the Consequences

After defining your distraction challenges, list the actions you currently take and assess your degree of productivity. Note the relationship between interruptions in your work/life and their negative consequences. Because distractions negatively affect many factors—memory, organization, planning, and emotions—their costs involve loss of time, energy, accuracy, and completeness.

For example, Traci discovered that by jotting notes on a chart, she was able to clarify her thoughts. That's when it dawned on her that if she continued her negative patterns, she'd fall behind, increase her frustration, and pay a hefty price.

Traci's Balance of Consequences Worksheet
Issue: Writing Technical Reports Late in the Day

	Positive Consequences	Negative Consequences
Short-term	Mornings; enjoy sleeping in a bit Late afternoons: talk to others, have a few laughs, and enjoy the camaraderie	Frustrated and stressed
Long-term	None	Falling behind and looking incompetent
Other issues		Feel a bit down; don't get enough done before leaving work

Using a chart like this provides Traci with concrete information about her feelings. In addition, when discussing her situation with her supervisors, the chart provides a vehicle for discussion about overall concerns and options. Plus it turns into an agenda item for the next team meeting: *How can we reduce the worst of the late-afternoon distractions?*

3. Set Realistic Goals

It's critical to start the change process with relevant and realistic goals. Otherwise, you set yourself up for failure. You are the general in charge of change; only you can overcome the negative effect of distraction. Without a conscious focus on achievable goals, it's easy to drift back into unproductive old habits. So ask questions like these: "If I could wave a magic wand, what would I like to happen? What's my dream? Realistically, what is doable at this time? What goals will help me reduce distractions and increase productivity? What is the first step?" Self-dialogue helps you recognize and deal with any emotions that might have blocked your intentions to change.

In Traci's case, given her understanding of the consequences of her behavior, she plans to go to work early two or three days a week and write technical reports when she feels alert.

How will you use the information you note to develop realistic goals for yourself? Start by creating pictures in your mind. Wave your magic wand and visualize possible goals and their results. If you have multiple goals, prioritize each according to possible positive and negative consequences. Then ask, "What work/life benefits are associated with each possible goal?"

Even the simplest list provides a handy way to set goals. In a Microsoft report, Americans "report being in love with to-do lists," with more than 76 percent of people responding that lists help them keep organized and reduce stress. In fact, nearly four in five Americans keep to-do lists (Microsoft, 2008). Your lists might be related to personal and household activities, work, home repairs/renovations, and new ideas. View each item on your list as a mini-goal. Take time to prioritize items and estimate the time needed for each one; then schedule time in your planner to complete them.

4. Take Action

Moving from intention to action challenges many people. Worries creep in: "What's the first step? What if I fail?" To combat these concerns, just begin. Start small, start simply, but start.

Once you start, introduce both routine and repetition to pave the way for change. For example, as an initial effort, think about one possible goal, and schedule times during the next week to work on it. List a few actions to start, and identify a resource or two you need.

> *Alan is a graphic artist who owns a Web design business and teaches at several community colleges. He's extremely creative but too often fails to complete old projects when new, interesting projects come along. In addition, he underestimates the actual time it takes to complete the final changes for projects. He rarely hires other artists to help with the tedious tasks inherent in complex or long-term projects.*
>
> *Currently, he is past due on several projects, and his clients are aggravated. So to serve as a visual reminder, he posts by his phone the following written commitment in bold capital letters.*

FROM _____ TO _____, I CAN ACCEPT NEW PROJECTS ONLY WHEN I SEND OUT THE FINAL DRAFTS OF CURRENT PROJECTS. I need to focus on completing current contracts to ensure cash flow and to maintain my professional image. If I don't complete two projects by ____, I will hire one of my colleagues to help me finish.

To avoid forgetting or postponing delivery on the promises you make, crafting a written statement shows the details and reflects your commitment. Why does it work? It makes you describe your goal and schedule the actions to help you achieve the desired outcome. In addition, you identify a reward to recognize your effort and progress toward your goal. This formalized commitment curbs procrastination and facilitates your move from intention to action.

5. *Monitor and Maintain Progress*

Whether they're generals or drill sergeants, soldiers need to know what and how close the target is. Similarly, if you want to attain your goal, you need clear, specific information about your target—your goal. Without feedback on your performance, it's easy for your enthusiasm to wane. Specific information about whether and when to maintain or modify your Plan of Attack will help you stay plugged in.

If you're like most people, keeping information in your head doesn't work. Days and amounts blur; you're not completely conscious (or mindful) of how your feelings, thoughts, and actions are interrelated. For best results, keep a written record. Consider your preferred learning style when designing its format. For example, a visual learner might enjoy monitoring progress by checking off items represented by pictures or icons. A word person might write notes in a journal. A number person might plot progress on a graph.

Joyce uses the following chart to monitor her "getting out of the house on time" routine.

Joyce's "Getting Out of the House on Time" Routine
Monday/Wednesday

Goal: To rise, have 1-1/2 to 2 hours to get ready for work, and leave the house on time on Mondays and Wednesdays.

Time	Activity	Check (if completed)	Comments
6:30 a.m.	Alarm, wake up, go to the bathroom, brush teeth		
6:45 a.m.	Go downstairs, put on timer, make coffee, get food and medication		
7:00 a.m.	Read, watch television, clean up, put in a load of laundry		
7:30 a.m.	Get dressed		
8:00 a.m.	Walk dog		
8:30 a.m.	Leave for work		
9:00 a.m.	Arrive at work		

What's Joyce's reward for getting out of the house on time? Finishing her work in a timely manner and then leaving her office on time, which allows ample time to get to the gym for a jazz/dance class in the afternoon.

Gathering specific, timely, and relevant information about your progress helps you stay on track and adjust when needed. If you don't achieve the rate of success you want, rather than abandoning your goal consider ways of altering your Plan of Attack. Use information and insights about your progress to decide what, when, and how to change your plan. Continue to use those strategies that help you; drop those that are ineffective.

For some, getting positive feedback on their progress keeps them engaged in their Plan of Attack over time. Even if they're not progressing at the desired rate, they realize they're on the right track. In such cases, the movement toward a goal or the completion of a task serves as its own reward. It even increases the desire to continue striving.

For others, however, concrete rewards or incentives are required to get started and stay on track. Changing their behavior can be so arduous, they need to recognize and reward their effort even before they actually achieve their goals. If this is true for you, take time to put a checkmark next to each small step you accomplish.

For decades, research has supported the principle that positive reinforcement contributes to desired behavior change (Kanfer and Goldstein, 1980). That's why your plan should include a number of positive consequences to recognize your effort. Be thoughtful and specific in stating your progress. For example, for each day or week during which you pursue your goal, put money aside for a special purchase or plan a special event contingent on meeting your goal.

Informal sharing can also provide a powerful incentive to maintain your efforts. You might enjoy telling others about your accomplishments through conversations, blogs, e-mails, or other social networks. Use such reinforcements as long as doing so doesn't take too much time away from your core tasks. You don't want a five-minute break to turn into a two-hour lark, when you find yourself saying, "I can't believe how much time I wasted!"

Whatever your incentive, you might slip or fail to make progress at times. At those moments, optimistically say, "I'll do better next time." Identify the difficulty and search for a solution, and then say, "I must remember that I can have a new beginning. I want to get back on track."

List the personal benefits or rewards that would spur you on as you progress toward your goal:

- Benefit or reward: _____

- Benefit or reward: _____

- Benefit or reward: _____

- Benefit or reward: _____.

Be sure to refer back to these often. They'll keep you motivated.

3

7 Strategies to Implement Your Plan

October 17, 1999

Yesterday, in New York City, cellist Yo-Yo Ma left his $2.5 million 18th-century cello in the trunk of a taxicab on his way to a hotel. Four hours later, it turned up unharmed at the Maria Cab Company in Queens. Mr. Ma reported that he was exhausted from playing at Carnegie Hall and forgot the cello when he left the cab. (Finkelstein, 1999)

April 12, 2010

Roberta Flack, the renowned singer of 1970s soul ballads, left a suitcase of CDs in the back seat of a New York taxi. It had both finished and unfinished material for a new album. Ms. Flack reported, "When I got out, I was so anxious to get inside [the building] because it was raining." Luckily, she had the cab receipt so she could locate the taxi and retrieve her material. (Grynbaum, 2010)

In both of these instances, distractions triggered by the Demons of Fatigue and Stress led to slippages in memory—and potentially disastrous outcomes. How can you avoid slips in memory, loss of items, and costly consequences when traveling or just living every day? You can benefit from having a variety of techniques at your fingertips. When you can readily employ them, you're highly likely to set up a plan to reduce the distractions you experience.

The following seven strategies stem from research studies shown to be effective for different needs, interests, and situations. Their use, singly or in combination, not only reduces distractions but improves attention, memory, and organization (Forsyth and Eifort, 2007; Baer, 2006; Boekaerts et al., 2005; Beck, 1995). The seven techniques are:

1. Visualization

2. Logic

3. Constructive self-talk

4. Positive assertiveness

5. Productive routines

6. Stop, Look, and Listen technique

7. Social support

Which technique you use first—or which ones you combine—depends on your natural talents and strengths. For example, if your skills lie in the visual area, try visualization first; if your strengths are in the verbal area, use self-talk. Consider which techniques—alone or in combination—might work best for you.

1. Use Visualization

This technique encourages you to use your mind's eye. Forming a mental image heightens your awareness and brings clarity and specificity about the situation or conditions that you confront. Winning elite athletes use visualization to simulate a competitive situation and mentally rehearse their moves. Research indicates that when you envision a problem and its possible solutions, you gain clarity and become empowered to regulate yourself and solve problems (Taylor, Pham, et al., 1998).

Practicing visualization can help you stop distractions and interruptions from sabotaging your work/life performance. Here's what to do:

- Create a mental movie of a situation in which you experience distractions.

- Play a few scenes, and use your mind's eye to pinpoint the challenges.

- Identify possible techniques to overcome the challenges you "see."

- Set a realistic, short-term goal for incorporating those techniques into your life.

When setting a goal, start by engaging in a visual rehearsal. Imagine the scene and ask, "To reach my goal, what is the likelihood of this technique working or not working?"

Like any other picture, a mental picture is worth a thousand words. By the same token, the use of concrete visual aids also enhances performance and memory. Making any kind of graphic representation requires attention and boosts organization. As an example, you could draw a timeline on a large board and mark the specific tasks required to achieve your goal on it, complete with start and end dates.

Action

Describe a situation in which you could use visualization to reduce distractions:

_____

_____

---

2. Use Reason

When others don't use their problem-solving skills well, it's probably obvious to you. You may react to their faulty thinking by saying, "That doesn't make sense," or "You're coming to the wrong conclusion." Commonly, it's easier to recognize faulty thinking in others than in yourself. However, you can realize benefits from monitoring your own problem-solving process, especially during heated situations. When you turn to reason rather than emotion to deal with difficulties, you present clear thoughts in an orderly sequence. If needed, you support your argument with evidence and deliver points that lead to a logical conclusion.

Almost twenty-four hundred years ago, Aristotle advised us to use rational thought to manage life. His philosophy can still guide you in dealing with current problems (Madvin and Markel, 2012). Contemporary psychologists have researched and proposed similar "reasoning" approaches. For example, Albert Ellis (2001) describes faulty thinking as the path to frustration and unhappiness. Like Aristotle, he advocates using rational thinking to defend against unreasonable requests—and preserve your mental health.

Faulty thinking not only impedes logical problem solving; it often blocks assertive behavior, especially when making or refusing requests that relate to distraction. When you give up the irrational belief that everyone should be like you—or give up believing you can avoid all conflict by not asking for what you need—you'll reduce the number of visits from the Stress Demon.

Mindfulness means paying attention in a particular way—having one purpose, being in the present moment, and being nonjudgmental (Kabat-Zinn, 1992; Miller et al.,

1995). One component of mindfulness is the knowledge that a thought is transitory— that is, thought doesn't necessarily reflect reality or connote a permanent state. Just because you think something doesn't mean the thought is true.

Understanding how your mind works and then using your powers of reasoning to reduce your vulnerability to distractions is worth practicing every day. Reason and rational thinking also contribute to realistic expectations. For example, you may be intelligent and have a strong auditory (listening) learning style. That means you might be receptive to learning through verbal, musical, or audio cues in general, but when you want to concentrate you may also be especially vulnerable to noise. If your pride gets the better of your logic, though, you might assume that because you're a capable person, you should be able to concentrate in any setting, even a noisy one. You hide your difficulties while imposing an unrealistic expectation on yourself, believing, "If I'm smart, I must be able to focus, no matter where I am." If the overstimulation gets the better of you, you might rationalize your negative feelings this way: "I didn't block out the noise, so I must be dumb and worthless." In such cases, the fear of not living up to your self-image gets in the way of using a logical, factual, realistic problem-solving approach.

Regardless of how intelligent you are, face it: at times, you simply won't be able to focus. Instead, identify your strengths as gifts, don't exaggerate your vulnerabilities or weaknesses, and simply accept the diversity that's inherent in our universe.

Action

Describe a situation in which you could use reason to reduce distractions:

_____

_____

---

3. Use Constructive Self-Talk

A voice in your head labels and judges events and feelings throughout the day and, sometimes, throughout the night. The messages you receive from these internal conversations can be positive or negative. With negative self-talk, you hear thoughts filled with shame, blame, self-doubt, or worry. Negative self-talk shows up in phrases like these: "I shouldn't do this," or "I mustn't think that," or "I won't be able to accomplish my goal." Messages like these inhibit positive, proactive problem-solving behavior; the glass is half empty.

Positive and constructive self-talk, however, quiet your inner critic. You hear messages filled with positive attributions and optimism, such as, "It's time to try a new approach," or "I will be satisfied to improve one step at a time." With messages like these, the glass is half full.

Everyone engages in self-talk, but some people barrage themselves with many more negative than positive messages. When you want to move from self-awareness to self-initiated action and regulation, you require positive statements. Indeed, you become your own cheerleader and problem solver. If you make a mistake or experience a mishap, then label it as such. Remember, it's a behavior or problem that needs a solution; it's not an indictment of your character. So refrain from calling yourself an idiot or labeling yourself as lazy. Instead of asking, "Why am I such a jerk?" change it and ask, "What is the better way?"

You'll find it's easier to develop positive interpretations of your behavior when you are mindful or conscious of both the conditions and the consequences surrounding it. For example, once you become aware that you make e-mail errors when you're fatigued, you can prevent mistakes by rearranging your schedule. If you fall into your old pattern, simply say, "I know better than to work when I'm tired. I need to take care of myself and work when I'm alert."

What you say to yourself definitely matters. Studies indicate that optimism is associated with better health, performance, and social success (Seligman, 1991; Lyubomirski, King, and Diener, 2005). When you feel positive and optimistic, you have energy available for creative thought, which paves the way for progress toward your goal. Bottom line: Don't distract yourself with negativity!

However, using positive and constructive self-talk doesn't mean you paint a rosy picture of all situations and deny the existence of difficulty. It does mean you problem solve—that is, you take on a positive view, make a plan, and use information about your progress to improve.

Action

Describe a situation in which you could use self-talk to reduce distractions:

_____

_____

---

4. Use Positive Assertiveness

Assertive behavior involves the ability to stand up for your rights without violating the rights of others (Alberti and Emmons, 2008).

Using assertive skills helps you avoid unnecessary distractions from one, or a combination, of the demons. For example, when you behave assertively, you recognize that being a caring, responsible person doesn't mean others can access your attention any time they want it, no matter how disruptive. As you might have experienced, granting others unlimited access usually invites overwhelming distraction disasters. Using positive assertiveness helps protect you from distraction, interruption, or overcommitment by the *Others* Demon. Assert yourself by stating you have the right to quiet time to think, and learn to say no nicely.

When you are assertive, you recognize your right to:

- Clear directions when assigned a task. It's difficult to begin a task when you're not sure about what to do and how it must be done. Frequently, procrastination results from this. Protect yourself from distractions created by the Activities Demon; demand specific instructions and standards.

- Work/life settings that are conducive to a positive atmosphere and your working style. Protect yourself from distractions created by the Spaces Demon; ask for the space, conditions, and supplies you need.

- Feelings expressed in a polite, courteous way. When you stifle your feelings, you're apt to experience stress, perhaps including ruminating about what you would have or could have said. Protect yourself from the angst of distractions created by the Stress Demon; appropriately share your feelings with the parties involved or, at the very least, write down your deep feelings in a diary or journal.

Action

Describe a situation in which you could use positive assertiveness to reduce distractions:

_____

_____

---

5. Set Productive Routines

Routines help establish effective work/life patterns while reducing the need to spend extra energy on behaviors you do repeatedly. For example, if you don't want to run around finding your keys, wallet, and glasses, then as soon as you arrive home, routinely place everything in a container or on a shelf by the door.

When you create a routine, you structure your time, space, and rate of action. Doing the same thing the same way, at the same time, increases the chances you can successfully ward off distractions. Routines, therefore, bolster your efforts to attain your goals.

Jean, who runs a home-based business, establishes a routine to ensure she exercises in the morning. She lists what she can and can't do before completing her workout. She knows that once she's distracted by e-mail or phone calls, she doesn't exercise, and she frets all day as she walks around in her workout clothes. She creates a list that helps her follow a routine that includes her exercise—and reduces her frustration about her lack of self-discipline. Jean's routine looks like this:

___ *Get up and put on exercise clothes. Do not brush teeth.*
___ *Go directly to the treadmill. Don't answer the phone or use the computer.*
___ *Record the mileage and time on the workout log posted by the treadmill.*
___ *Congratulate self; smile and say, "Good job!"*
___ *Brush teeth, shower, and dress*
___ *Get coffee and breakfast*
___ *Take several deep breaths, stretch, and start to work*

Writing a list or planning your activities brings any problem into sharper focus, in line with the old saying, "If it's worth thinking about, it's worth writing about." Remember, the act of writing is conscious; it makes you focus and brings clarity. Be sure to include writing in your routine.

Action

Describe a situation in which you could use a productive routine to reduce distractions:

_____

_____

---

6. Use the Stop, Look, and Listen Technique

The Stop, Look, and Listen technique involves several modalities and steps. Use this handy technique when you slip up or feel tired, ill, or stressed—also when you're preoccupied about a life circumstance. Remember that even a positive event, such as a vacation or wedding, can trigger feelings of fatigue and stress.

The Stop, Look, and Listen technique ensures you're attentive when completing important personal and financial tasks or doing dangerous activities, such as using power tools or driving heavy equipment.

Here is the routine:

- *Stop*: Take a timeout for half a minute or even a few minutes. Allow your mind and body to relax and refocus on the task.

- *Look*: Visualize the situation. Be vigilant about the conditions under which you are to perform or complete a task. What materials do you need? What are possible dangers or pitfalls?

- *Listen*: Engage in constructive self-talk, providing instructions about what to do or not do. You'll find that when you give yourself directions, you focus more sharply and listen more carefully. In addition, you reduce the chances of distraction from outside noises or intrusive thoughts.

The Stop, Look, and Listen technique is a refreshing strategy you can employ any time of the day!

Action

Describe a situation in which you could use Stop, Look, and Listen to reduce distractions:

_____

_____

---

7. Seek Social Support

Humans are social animals, and evidence backs the idea that social support helps people deal with difficulties and change (Vaux, 1988). Sharing your successes as well as your difficulties helps you to stay focused and identify alternatives if need be.

You can find social support by turning to family, friends, peers, or experts in your life. As you embark on your battle plan against distraction, identify a few people who will provide a listening ear or helping hand. This kind of support can go a long way to positively affecting your mental well-being.

Commonly, you enjoy emotional support when you have a sense of belonging, feel cared for, talk over a problem, or gain encouragement. During emotionally trying times or major life transitions, social support might include giving or receiving money, housing, transportation, or childcare. When life is tough, it's not only nice but *necessary* to share the burden. Being open to giving and receiving also reduces the distractions triggered by worry and uncertainties.

Even when you're making contracts with yourself, tell trusted friends or colleagues about your commitments. When you share information and your feelings about the focus-killers in your life, they become less lethal.

Action

Describe a situation in which you could use social support to reduce distractions:

_____

_____

The seven research-based strategies above help you reduce distractions and improve attention, memory, and organization. Most likely, you know your preferences well. You might prefer to follow a sequence of steps and try every strategy. Or you might choose to select and experiment with one step or strategy at a time. Whatever your style, decide when and how to employ these strategies—and reap the rewards of clear-mindedness.

Be Your Mind's Chief of Staff

Our bodies and minds seek pleasure or comfort; they strive to avoid pain. Therefore, to change a behavior, you need to make it as painless as possible. Try to be your mind's chief of staff, creating ways to use your interests and creativity to "invite" yourself into the experience. For example, if you're a sports fanatic, identify with a favorite player or athlete. If you're artistic, draw and create visually appealing contracts, charts, or checklists.

Most important, understand how, when, and where to use your attention skills. Apply some or all of the research-based strategies from this chapter to accomplish your behavior-changing goals. Take one step at a time, and move from intention to action.

THE TECHNOLOGY DEMON

The Technology Demon is on the prowl day and night.
It invites us to get lost in a maze of texting, chatting,
surfing, and gaming long after it's appropriate or useful.

4

Actions Against the Technology Demon

Author Jonathan Franzen, whose newest novel is hailed by critics as "brilliant," announced to the audience at a reading in London that a draft version of his book Freedom had been published by mistake. Oops! Somehow, someone opened and copied the wrong file rather than the one with the final revisions. Over eight thousand copies of the almost six-hundred-page book were published. Ironically, his previous award-winning book was entitled The Corrections (Davis, 2010; Daily Mail Reporter, 2010).

Can you imagine the chagrin and expense involved in this error? We're not privy to the distraction that caused this oops, but we can conclude that no one is immune from distraction, not even the best and the brightest. Inattention causes errors or inefficiencies that can plague us in all aspects of life.

Reports indicate a high cost for technology-related inattentiveness in the workplace. In monetary terms, interruptions from technology (and other people) cost our economy $997 billion (Spira, 2010). Another report revealed, "Interruptions consume a little over two hours a day, or 28 percent of the workday" (Spira and Feintuch, 2005).

When working devices are used, their sights or sounds distract you. When devices don't work, you're irritated. Too frequently, the Technology Demon erodes your productivity and escalates work/life stress. In addition, distractions caused by a chirping cell phone or fiddling with an iPod can trigger accidents when driving, biking, or even walking. Beware of the constant, profound, and insidious effects of digital distractions throughout the day.

How can you reduce the constant distractions triggered by technology? This chapter addresses such issues as multitasking, safety, and security issues. It also provides charts, checklists, and tips to help you take action against distractions while you use technology at work and at home.

The Tyranny of the Technology Demon

The types and numbers of technology devices that demand our attention in our world have exploded. The usual amounts of business correspondence, e-mail, and telephone calls increase exponentially. Many average businesspeople in the workplace complain of being overwhelmed and frustrated by a constant, unstoppable flow of stimuli, information, and opportunities.

How about those individuals who, by nature, are more vulnerable to distractions? And those who easily get bored? They fall prey to devices like cell phones or Personal Digital Assistants (PDAs), especially when the device houses favorite entertainment or information applications.

You likely know people who are psychologically tied to these gadgets; they feel naked and lost unless they have some such gadget in their hands. Besides showing rudeness toward others they're with, people who overuse gadgets waste time and energy. The etiquette of using cell phones and PDAs has become a cultural topic, discussed in published articles like "Should You Google at Dinner?" (Feiler, 2010). And the rapid rise of social media entices users to check Facebook, Twitter, LinkedIn, Pinterest or other accounts "just for a moment." Unfortunately, it's never *just* a moment.

Because of technology, we continually operate using partial attention, but high-order thinking requires our full attention. We need to keep information in focus so we can remember, sequence, and rearrange that information when making decisions and solving problems. In addition, rest and relaxation require uninterrupted time that allows us to *calm down* or *gear up* as needed during the day.

What a paradoxical situation! On one hand, we need technology to conduct business and personal affairs. On the other hand, if we fail to be cautious and disciplined, the tool we depend on subverts our efforts to perform with speed and accuracy. When overused or abused, the technology we rely on disrupts our thinking, wastes our time, leads to inaccuracies—and fosters stress as a result. It takes conscious effort and proven strategies to deal with these technology challenges.

Do you feel helpless against the pull *away* from work *toward* the distracting aspects of technology? Whether in the form of e-mails, cell phones, or social networks, the Technology Demon can be today's greatest enemy of top performance and high productivity. To what degree are you tyrannized by technology?

Self-Check: The Technology Demon

Read each statement under Activity and check all that apply to you. Then visualize events that occurred over the last few days and estimate the number of times a day you were distracted or interrupted. Write down that estimate for each question that applies.

	Activity	**Times per Day**
___	1. I misplace or lose devices, such as a cell phone, PDA, iPod, iPad or tablet.	___
___	2. I waste money by overusing shopping, gaming, or gambling websites.	___
___	3. I am interrupted and sometimes feel overwhelmed by the chirping or ringing of cell phones and alerts from tweets, e-mails, or text messages.	___
___	4. I waste time using social networks, surfing the Internet, or playing games.	___
___	5. I am distracted while driving when using my cell phone or device.	___
___	6. I rarely use security and backup procedures for my computer or other devices.	___
___	7. I don't have an organized system for storing manuals, passwords, logins, or technical support information.	___
___	8. I rarely schedule time to organize or delete old messages or files.	___
___	9. I have trouble keeping track of paraphernalia, such as chargers and cords.	___
___	10. I forget to schedule regular maintenance for equipment, software, or virus-scanning updates.	___

If you checked more than one or two items, then the Technology Demon may be inhibiting your efficiency. By understanding that better technology management yields higher productivity and reduces stress, you can get a handle on digital distractions. Once you identify the ways in which the Technology Demon interferes with your productivity, take stock of the number and types of devices you have. If you don't already have them on file, jot down the model and serial number for each device. During the process, be sure to ask these two questions:

- How many devices are too many?

- Can I pare down the number of gadgets and reduce the distractions they impose?

General Consequences of the Technology Demon

Countless numbers of people are momentarily caught and succumb to distraction; they suffer the consequences of technology gone awry—including people in high places, as this example shows.

> *Gordon Brown, England's former prime minister, attests to the humiliating and costly consequences of distraction when using even the most innocuous piece of equipment. He failed to shut off a live microphone after a pre-election debate. His ungracious remarks about an encounter with a member of the audience were replayed across the world on the Internet, blogs, and newscasts. How much this incident played into his lost election is not known, but it certainly did not help. (Lyall, 2010)*

Even though Prime Minister Brown had assistants to anticipate slipups and smooth the way, this political leader paid a price for his lack of vigilance with technology. Since the networks can spread remarks instantly throughout the world, everyone needs to be vigilant, especially when they're vulnerable to distraction.

Everyone grapples with the question, "Does our digital world help or hinder our ability to pay attention?" People debate about if and how we suffer from Divided Attention Disorder (DAD). This term refers to "a state of affairs whereby we're pulled from pillar to post by the overwhelming connectivity of modern technology" (Orlowski, 2011).

Mostly, people tend to ignore or deny the insidious effects of the Technology Demon. Isn't it time to assess how you let technology split your attention on a regular basis?

Assess: Keep a Technology Journal

How frequently do you misplace, misuse, or overuse a technical device? Sometimes you spend too many hours on the Internet, while other times you burn too many cell phone minutes talking, texting, or tweeting. Have you ever missed a deadline because you wasted time on the phone or Internet? As you slip further into bad technology habits, you'll find that time flies and money evaporates. That's why it's critical to keep track of your use (and possible abuse) of devices by completing My Technology Journal.

My Technology Journal

Device	Amount of Time Spent Daily	Amount of Money Spent Monthly/ Yearly	Frustrating Incident(s)	Lessons Learned
Cell Phone				
E-mail				
Social Networking				
Internet Browsing				
Gaming, Gambling, or Shopping				
Other				

Take time to become mindful of how technology triggers distraction for you. Address questions such as:

- What are my most common triggers for distraction by the Technology Demon?

- When, where, and how is the technology having a negative effect on my attention?

- What am I currently doing to manage technology? In what ways are my solutions working? What are my feelings about these situations?

Analyze Personal Consequences

When you use a journal, you gain insight about the depth of possible problems. You also gain insight about your patterns and can more clearly "see" the consequences of your behavior.

To analyze the personal consequences of your behavior, you might ask:

- Exactly how many hours do I spend on unnecessary social networking?

  Best guess: _____ hours a week

- How often do I misplace my cell phone or iPod?

  Best guess: _____ times a week

- How much time (plus money and frustration) do I waste using devices inappropriately?

  Best guess: _____ amount per week

- How serious are technology distractions at my work, home, and elsewhere? Evaluate by using a scale from one to ten, with ten indicating the most serious consequences.

Work:	1	2	3	4	5	6	7	8	9	10
Home:	1	2	3	4	5	6	7	8	9	10
Other:	1	2	3	4	5	6	7	8	9	10

Your answers tell you a lot about the use, overuse, or abuse of technology. So what can you do to improve the situation?

Set Realistic Goals to Tame the Technology Demon

First, assess your current technology practices and analyze their consequences. From there, you can foster a commitment to change any unproductive habits. Although you might say, "I'm going to spend less time than I normally do on the cell phone or Internet," it's hard to do. Setting small, simple goals can facilitate your progress. Your goals could include:

- Avoid using all devices or gadgets for fifteen to twenty minutes a day; instead, engage in analytical, creative, or recreational activities. If twenty minutes isn't realistic, what amount of time is? However long the time, schedule quiet think time into your calendar. If necessary, set an alarm to alert you to start.

- Increase the number of breaks you take while working on your computer, including breaks to rest your tired eyes and move your body.

- Arrange for offsite storage of files, data, and photos to minimize the risk of losing them to the Technology Demon.

Right now, review your weekly schedule to identify a small, simple goal for reducing your vulnerability to technology-related distractions. Note what you will do or say to ensure you have quality think time.

- At work _____

- At home _____

- Other setting _____

Major Strategy: Impose an *Electronic Lockdown*

Too often, days are plagued with overwhelming distractions from the technology that's supposed to help you. You end up with less time available for high-quality planning and creative thought. So limit the stimuli that affect your functioning. Remember, for thousands of years societies achieved wondrous feats without modern technology. You can too—at least for brief periods.

To develop a productive habit, impose a temporary *electronic lockdown* and unleash your psychic energy. Turn off your computer, phone, beeper, television, iPad, and/or iPod. See how much more work you can complete when you think through problems in a non-distracting setting. Some people declare digital-free days, taking a break from the never-ending electronic intrusions. As a result, they create a greater sense of peace and satisfaction.

Use the following calendar to schedule protected, quiet think time. Indicate the times you'll impose an *electronic lockdown* to free yourself from distraction and interruption. You don't have to schedule a full hour; you'll be surprised how much you can enhance your productivity with a digital disconnection lasting only fifteen to twenty minutes. Schedule it now.

Weekly Calendar

Hours	Sunday	Monday	Tuesday	Wednesday	Thursday	Friday	Saturday
6 a.m.							
7 a.m.							
8 a.m.							
9 a.m.							
10 a.m.							
11 a.m.							
12 a.m.							
1 p.m.							
2 p.m.							
3 p.m.							
4 p.m.							
5 p.m.							
6 p.m.							
7 p.m.							
8 p.m.							
9 p.m.							
10 p.m.							
11 p.m.							
12 a.m.							
1 a.m.							

Issue and Strategies: Distracted Driving

"Dnt Txt N Drv" is a plea by Oprah Winfrey, who described the difficulty of changing a dangerous habit in a *New York Times* article (Winfrey, 2010). Driver inattention factors into more than one million crashes in North America annually, resulting in serious injuries and deaths. The economic impact reaches nearly forty billion dollars annually (AAA, 2011). Know that you'll likely quadruple your risk of crashing when you use a cell phone while driving.

No one denies the problem and its potential dangers. According to one study, nearly 90 percent of drivers considered texting or e-mailing a serious threat, and 58 percent said talking on the phone while driving posed another serious threat to their safety. Many of the same people admitted they had texted, e-mailed, or talked on their cell phone while driving (AAA Foundation, 2009).

Like many, you realize the dangers to yourself and others when you allow a cell phone or other device to prevent you from keeping your full focus on the road. What about you? Are you tempting the fates?

Most people need to consciously reduce distractions and stop multitasking while driving. How? Consider these options:

- Tell others you will not use your cell phone when you're driving.

- Leave your phone on the back seat or somewhere you can't reach it.

- Pull over if you must make or answer a call on your cell phone.

Visualize or review your weekly schedule and write a small, simple goal for reducing your use of technology when driving.

My goal is to: _____

Issue and Strategies: The Evil Empire of E-mail

Many in business feel overwhelmed by the need to respond to the fifty, seventy-five, or more e-mails they receive each day. You might even feel acute pressure and shame because you can't keep up with the barrage of messages you receive. Bleary-eyed, you may feel as if you're drowning in a sea of messages. When you take time off, the number of messages rises at an astounding rate. Estimates indicate that 294 billion e-mails are sent each day, although about 75 percent of that number is spam (Radicati Group, 2011). How many e-mails do you receive a day? How often do alerts from your e-mail, Skype, or social media contacts interrupt you? How much time do you waste satisfying your curiosity by clicking links listed in your e-mails and finding out who links to whom?

As with other aspects of technology, consider e-mail a two-edged sword. As a tool, it's essential for conducting your personal and business affairs. At the same time, e-mail increases pressure, wastes time, and diverts (as well as dissipates) your psychic energy. It's critical to adopt a variety of strategies to stop the deluge of useless e-mail and manage only the necessary ones.

How? Calculate the amount of time you devote to e-mail each day. Then calculate how much time you would gain for relaxing, exercising, and doing other tasks if you reduced that time by at least 10 percent. Ask, "For each day or week, how much communication do I really need? How much is too much?"

Use visualization to reframe the problem. View e-mail as you would other communication and impose clear directions and boundaries. Few people think it's okay to allow unopened US mail to pile high for weeks, even months. At the least, they separate the crucial, time-sensitive, official-looking mail from flyers and solicitations.

Engage in an internal dialogue and ask, "Am I complicating my life by not deleting messages? Do I harbor the fear that I'll need them sometime? Do I waste time on nonessential correspondence?" Identify exactly how you spend your e-mail time.

Armed with that information, assertively exert control. Stop wasting time on nonessential e-mail and manage the essential flow of correspondence more efficiently. You're processing a constant flow of information, but you can stem the tide of e-mail problems by committing to action and selecting strategies to do so. Start by checking any tips listed here that you'd like to implement.

___ Be ruthless. Immediately delete and unsubscribe from any unwanted newsletter or announcement feeds.

___ Establish a decision-making system by deciding what actions are warranted for each message: e.g., delete, archive, file by category for response at a later date, schedule as a work task, read and respond to immediately.

___ Organize. Create a filing system and use color-coded tags to store or archive categories of e-mail (e.g., travel, legal, committees, or organizations).

___ Be timely. Schedule fifteen- to thirty-minute periods to prioritize and schedule tasks first thing in the morning or the night before.

___ Postpone. Put low priority materials, such as newsletters, reports, or teleseminars, in a folder and schedule a limited weekly time to review them.

___ Use the subject line to summarize your message to make it easier for others to process your mail. Ask them to do the same when they send you e-mails.

___ Use a kitchen timer. Even on the weekends, allow yourself only a specific period to deal with e-mail. And stick with it!

___ Use social support. Discuss the problem with peers and family; with their help, identify ways to deal with time-wasting e-mails.

___ Avoid using your e-mail inbox as a to-do list. Instead, as soon as you see a task that needs doing, schedule time on your calendar to work on it.

Issue and Strategies: Gaming Addictions

Paula, a highly intelligent and competent civil servant, admits to overusing computer games. Initially providing a benign break for her, online solitaire has become a time-waster and source of guilt. Paula admits she often spends hours playing at work when she should be writing reports. Is she addicted to online gaming or does she just have a bad habit?

Studies estimate that 10 to 15 percent of gamers exhibit excessive and compulsive behavior and thus would meet the World Health Organization's criteria for addiction. Like others who have various addictions, they experience loss of time, money, energy, and productivity at work, home, or school.

Now more than ever, easy access to games through cell phones provides greater opportunities to overuse or abuse games. For example, in more than thirty countries, the number-one application for the iPhone, iPad, and iTouch is the game called Angry Birds, designed by Ravio in 2009, with more than five hundred million copies downloaded worldwide. In the game, players seek revenge over the green pigs who stole the birds' eggs. Designed for use in smartphones, it has over 150 levels and can be played while on the go or standing in line. As one reporter said, "The game is easy to learn and hard to stop playing" (Warthan, 2010).

If you or someone you know drifts into addictive habits, reach out and deal with the difficulty. Be assertive, direct, and honest, and deliver a positive message and a list of resources available for this problem (such as www.video-game-addiction.org).

Visualize or review your weekly schedule and write a small, simple goal for reducing the use, overuse, or abuse of surfing, gaming, gambling, shopping, or related online activities.

My goal is to: _____

Issues and Strategies: Organizing and Maintaining Equipment

When dealing with technology, adopt two basic habits that will increase your productivity. The first habit involves organizing equipment, manuals, peripherals, and other information. The second habit addresses regular maintenance of hardware and software.

For the first habit, establish a systematic way of storing and accessing your equipment to avoid loss of time and increased stress. Adopt the way that's easiest for you. For example, Phyllis writes key information pertaining to her equipment in a spiral-bound address book. She ties one side of a red string to the spiral and attaches the other side to her desk drawer knob. Without a string, she knows she'd misplace it or bury the information under a pile of papers. Herb, on the other hand, stores his information on an Excel spreadsheet on his home computer and backs up the file on an external drive.

Review the following list of organizational techniques and check those you'd consider using. Each one can serve as a mini-goal.

____ Create an organized method for storing and accessing equipment. Label all cords, gadgets, and peripheries. Consider using a hanging shoe organizer to store light equipment, accessories, and manuals. Each shelf holds a different piece of equipment, such as a camera, video recorder, and related paraphernalia. If you have additional equipment, such as MP3 recorder, wireless microphone, laser pointers, batteries, and/or chargers, store them there.

____ Create a system for storing manuals and information. When a tech problem occurs, you don't want to scurry around trying to locate the manual and installation software or tech support, model, or registration numbers. Keep warrantees, manuals, and installation discs in easily accessible files. Some use a file drawer, while others prefer an pleated accordion file.

____ Record e-mail addresses, logins, passwords, and answers to privacy questions in an easily accessible place so you'll have the information you need when you need it. Also record the data for the five devices you use most often. Keep this information in a locked place, or give it to someone you trust for safekeeping.

____ Hope for the best, but plan for the worst. In case of an emergency, tell at least one trusted person the important passwords and security information for various personal accounts and records. Develop a chart or spreadsheet to convey pertinent information about your e-mails, social networks, banks, organizations, and stores. Also record such information as the names of organizations you belong to, their addresses and phone numbers, your member number, login, and password, and the answer to privacy questions for each.

For the second habit, take responsibility for learning how to care for equipment and make minor repairs. Have on-call technical support numbers posted for software difficulties, and find a reliable technical support person. Are you lucky enough to have a friend like Mitch, alias the Computer Wizard? A retired physicist and faculty member, Dr. Rycus loves to tinker with technology. He helps the unsophisticated soul move through today's increasingly complex computer mazes. He even makes house calls. To keep up with your technological needs, cajole, barter with, or hire someone like Dr. Rycus to help you.

How can you keep your technology mess and stress at a minimum? Review this list and check any that you can embrace as a mini-goal or call to action.

___ Allot time each week/month to update your software programs.

___ Learn a little bit every week. Sometimes you experience software problems due to misunderstanding and misuse. Read the instructions, and practice. Skip trial and error; it's usually the least effective and most time-consuming way to learn.

___ Take a course, get an easy-to-read manual, call a friend, or use technical support services to continually upgrade your skills and deal with problems. Before buying a manual, review a number of books for the format, writing style, and illustrations that aid in your learning.

___ Ask to talk to a supervisor if your company's support technician can't solve your problem.

___ Keep a log of common problems and solutions.

___ Evaluate expenses. For example, do you spend your money wisely on new products and services? What ways can you cut costs?

___ Ask a friend to teach you a new piece of software, join a community-based class at a library or community college, or collaborate with a friend. Get support.

Visualize or review your weekly schedule to write a small, simple goal for increasing your ability to organize and maintain your equipment.

Use Demon-Defying Strategies

Situation: You keep putting off the mundane, tedious task of listing all your passwords in a protected file separate from your computer. Check those strategies that might help you to act on your own behalf.

___ *Use visualization.* Imagine forgetting your computer or PDA in a taxi. Someone gets into your e-mail and bank account. Feel the stress. Commit to an action that will prevent that from happening.

___ *Use reason.* Be aware of the negative results you may experience. Say, "If I don't protect myself from fraud, identity theft, or loss of my data, it will be a mess, and perhaps very costly. I need to act consciously on my own behalf."

___ *Use constructive self-talk.* Everyone feels rushed and often neglects chores. Say, "Protection isn't a nicety, it's a necessity. I need to schedule at least one fifteen-minute period every week to do this right."

___ *Use positive assertiveness.* Insist that people you're responsible for give you access to their login and password information in case of an emergency.

___ *Set productive routines.* The risk of identity theft or data loss requires your close attention to protection and privacy. Take action on the following suggestions:

- Schedule a time to password-protect the data on your computer, cell phone, or PDA and then schedule times when you'll change all passwords.

- Identify a separate device or company to provide offsite storage of data and schedule times when you will archive photos or other files. For example, you can use an external drive or memory sticks. You can also turn to Internet storage services, such as LastPass (https://www.lastpass.com) or iCloud (http://www.apple.com/icloud/) for backing up your critical information.

- Identify trustworthy people who you can give the login and password for your e-mail, cell phone, and other online accounts in case you're in an accident or otherwise unable to act on your own behalf.

___ *Use the Stop, Look, and Listen technique.* Stop and schedule a time every week to ensure your privacy is protected. Periodically purge or archive your files. Sort through the e-mails, phone numbers, and text messages that can be deleted—and just do it!

- Identify the times of the day, week, or month when you'll permanently delete *old and unnecessary* temporary Internet files, items in your recycle bin, trash from your e-mail account or cell phone, and others.

___ *Seek social support.* Call a friend, family member, colleague, or other resource and coordinate times to do your "technology chores." Some people use such Internet video services as Skype or iChat to work on such tasks. Remember, much can be accomplished in twenty-minute work sessions.

Moving from Intention to Action

Moving from good intention to positive action requires focusing on these steps to tame the Technology Demon:

1. *Assess.* Visualize work/life activities in which your productivity is lagging due to technology-driven distractions. Ask, "How is the Technology Demon interfering with my performance or sense of satisfaction?" Write down your answers.

2. *Analyze consequences.* List the costs and consequences of technology-driven distractions related to your work/life activities. Estimate the time, money, or energy you waste because of these distractions. Ask, "As I try to complete my daily activities, to what degree is distraction interfering with my productivity, diminishing my image, or wasting my time or money?" Review the possible positives. Estimate the gains you can realize if you reduce distractions, and write them down.

3. *Set realistic goals.* Visualize ways that would help you move toward more positive consequences. Ask, "What are one or two goals to decrease distractions and increase my performance when I'm engaged in important work/life technology-related activities?"

4. *Take action.* Identify strategies to remove or decrease technology distractions at

work or at home. Ask, "When, where, and how will I move from intention to action?" and "What specific strategies or tips will I use?"

_____

_____

5. *Monitor and maintain progress.* The more frequently you reward and recognize your efforts to stop a distracting behavior like texting all day, the easier it is keep yourself going in the right direction. Ask, "How will I track progress toward my goal? What rewards or incentives can I access to sustain motivation? How can I deal with barriers or other demons? What resources or experts might I consider if I have questions or need support?"

_____

_____

Monitoring Actions Against the Technology Demon

	At Work	At Home	Other Setting
Impose an *electronic lockdown* for at least 15–20 minutes per day.			
Make a commitment *never* to text while driving.			
Assign one day a week when you will digitally disconnect to increase your digital downtime.			
Arrange for offsite storage of important irreplaceable files, data, or photographs in case of fire or theft.			
Schedule times to label all such portable equipment as a cell phone or laptop with return information in case of loss or mishap.			
Designate a few technology-free zones. Make a commitment like, "I will not use gadgets in restaurants or banks."			
Other:			

Marshal's Technology Success Story

Marshal depends on his Smart Phone for business and personal purposes. He feels a bit awkward with his device but uses it constantly. However, he also has a healthy distrust of the various devices that have betrayed him at one time or another. When Marshal upgrades to a newer model, naively, he attempts to transfer the data from his computer to the new PDA using the sync function. He's aghast when he realizes that the new device has completely overridden the old database on the computer, leaving him with no data. After the initial shock subsides, he remembers that when his brother last visited, they took the time to back up the data on a CD and make a hard copy of the address book. This reinforced his belief in regularly backing up and filing all critical files, including data from e-mails, mobile phones, and cameras.

For Marshal, a preemptive strike warded off the disastrous effects of lost data and invasion of privacy. Rather than wait for a catastrophic event, he turned to the support of an experienced family member to complete a task he might have otherwise neglected.

THE OTHERS DEMON

The Others Demon has many faces: co-workers, bosses, significant others, and/or children who feel we should be available 24/7. When we can't stop interruptions, set boundaries, or say no, opportunities for creativity are lost.

5

Actions Against the Others Demon

When Marco is hired, he's assigned to a tiny, closet-sized office—at least it's quiet. The next thing he knows, cost-cutting requires that Gwen, his supervisor, share the space with him. The back of Gwen's chair continually bumps into Marco's. Her loud telephone voice constantly entertains callers, both business and personal. At times, Gwen leans over Marco's shoulder, peers at his computer screen, and badgers him with questions like, "What are you working on? Why are you spending time on that now?" But the worst? Gwen eats smelly fast-food sandwiches for lunch and then suffers from indigestion. Burps, belches, and other indications of intestinal distress punctuate every afternoon.

Marco feels caught in a distraction dungeon. He's unable to concentrate, and his productivity slows down; as the work piles up, so does the stress. He's so agitated and aggravated by his supervisor, he can't feel satisfaction even when he completes a task.

Marco isn't alone in dealing with a distracting coworker. According to reports, "We get interrupted from what we are doing an average of nine times per hour. Such interruptions are frustrating since you lose your train of thought, slow down, and stop your flow of energy or creativity" (Wechsler, 2009).

How can you protect yourself from numerous interruptions posed by family, friends, coworkers, or even people online, through e-mail and social networks? This chapter provides helpful charts, checklists, and tips for taking action against distractions triggered by others. Distractions include bullying, faulty thinking, and caring for the caregiver.

Invasion of the *Others* Demon

Too frequently, those nearest and dearest to you present the most distractions. Your family or friends may lack sensitivity about your need for uninterrupted time. Whether working at the office or home, your inner voice might scream, "Leave me alone so I can think!"

Sometimes you face a situation I call "the helping hand strikes again." Others kindly want to help, but they distract you all day and all night. For example, Martha stays home to finish writing the last chapters of her book. During the day, friends and family call or stop by "just for a minute." At night, her husband asks, "How are you doing? Do you want anything? When will you be done?"

Ironically, you can use the social support of others to help you manage the *Others* Demon, as did Martha's friend, who saved the day. She invited Martha to work in her apartment, which became Martha's sanctuary.

How often do others distract you and decrease the quantity and quality of your productivity? If your answer is "too often," then you're ready to exert control—and you have more choices than you think. First, become more mindful of the number and type of intrusions that sabotage your work. Once you recognize that, you can form a Plan of Attack to avert the continuing onslaught of the *Others* Demon.

Self-Check: The *Others* Demon

Directions: Read each of the following statements and place a check beside any that apply to you. Visualize events that occurred over the last few days and then write next to each statement your best guess of the average number of times a day you were distracted or interrupted.

____ 1. I get distracted when others interrupt me.   _____

____ 2. I get distracted by others' calls, texts, or e-mail.   _____

____ 3. I get interrupted by the noises made by others' gadgets.   _____

____ 4. I get distracted by people requesting help.   _____

____ 5. I get distracted by difficult (or bullying) people.   _____

____ 6. I get distracted when others wander by or approach me at work.   _____

____ 7. Other _____   _____

If you have checked more than a few of items, it's critical to tell those involved how they can help you reduce distraction and increase task completion. Completing a list like this gives you enough basic information to take action and delve deeper if you choose.

Another strategy is to keep a journal or diary. Simply write down your feelings and reactions to the distractions others "inflict" on you. Identify times when you must be free from distractions. List what you do and don't want from specific people, and then insist they respect your right to peace and quiet. Be assertive. Make choices like wearing earplugs or even moving your chair to face the wall.

General Consequences of the *Others* Demon

Research underscores how damaging interruptions in the workplace can be to one's productivity. Distractions from coworkers are among the top five reasons for wasting time, according to one survey (*Journal of Accountancy*, 2009). For each distraction, assess its intensity. Is it momentary (you can easily return to work) or is it a show-stopper (requires energy to backtrack, refocus, and recommit to the task)? For example, mental work on the computer places high demands on thinking and concentration. Not only might the quality of your effort be compromised by interruptions, but your level of stress tends to increase with each one. What are the consequences? The answer depends on the number of interruptions, the length of time they last, and the complexity of the task itself. So when the potential for interruptions by others exists, promptly discuss the situation with them; together, devise ways to neutralize any disturbances.

Assess: A Closer Look at Distractions Triggered by Others

When you collect information about the kinds and number of distractions triggered by others, you pinpoint problems and can plan a counterattack. So get specific. List the people who represent the most distractions at work or home. Next, list where, when, and how frequently these distractions occur.

Others **Distraction Chart**

Who Distracted You?	What Happened?	Where Did it Happen?	When Did it Happen?	Why Do You Think it Happened?	What Was the Effect on Your Work?

Become aware of how others trigger distraction for you, and address such questions as:

- What are my most common triggers for distraction by others?

  _____

  _____

  _____

- When, where, and how are others having a negative effect on my attention?

  _____

  _____

  _____

- What am I currently doing to manage the interruptions and distractions of others? In what ways are my solutions working? How do I feel about these situations?

  _____

  _____

  _____

Personal Consequences of the *Others* Demon

How much time, energy, or accuracy do you lose due to interruptions imposed by others? For example, you may not be fully aware of how time-consuming social networks like Facebook, LinkedIn, Twitter or Pinterest can be. Do the hours you spend on social networks encroach on time you need for work and for healthy activities like sleep and exercise?

Taking a closer look at the conditions and consequences related to the *Others* Demon puts you in a better position to become more efficient. Spend time reviewing your notes on how interruptions affect your productivity. Does the eighty/twenty rule apply in this situation—that is, are 20 percent of those you interact with accountable for 80 percent of the interruptions? Were those interruptions worth your time?

Describe the negative health, performance, or social consequences you experience. In this chart, rate the degree of negative consequences, using a scale from one to ten (with ten being the highest degree).

Identifying Negative Consequences of the *Others* Demon

Situations in Which You are Distracted by Others	Negative Health Consequences	Negative Productivity Consequences	Negative Social Consequences
1.			
2.			
3.			

Review the number and type of negative consequences and then consider the positive side. Use your notes on the chart to think about your goals.

Set Realistic Goals to Thwart the *Others* Demon

It's important to assess the consequences imposed by others. Consider doing some or all of the following to reduce the impact of others' distractions.

___ Post a sign or other notice to protect your think time for at least twenty minutes a day.

___ Send others a message that tells them you need fewer interruptions and more think time.

___ Schedule times for creative or analytical thought in an isolated place.

Visualize and review your weekly schedule. Identify a small, simple goal to help you reduce your vulnerability to the distractions of others. What will you say or do to ensure your right to undistracted think time?

- At work _____

- At home _____

- Other settings _____

Major Strategy: Positive Assertive Behavior

Whenever you need to concentrate and complete a task, remember that you have legitimate rights and responsibilities. For example, one right involves the opportunity to work in a undistracted setting, without interruptions from others. Your responsibilities include your conscious, committed action to arrange conditions so you can complete tasks effectively and efficiently.

Boosting your assertiveness actually requires tactics and practice (Alberti and Emmons, 2008). Stand up for your right to undisturbed time with these actions:

- Recognize it's okay to speak up and defend your right to protected think time.

- Learn the basic skills; it's not necessarily what you say, it's how you say it.

- Work to overcome obstacles, including your own inhibitions.

- Practice your new skills in nonthreatening situations—alone or with a trusted friend, professional, or coach.

Want to know an effective way to decrease the distracting behavior of others? Catch them being helpful. That's it. Draw attention to the positive behaviors of others that support your need for less distraction. Tell those people why their actions worked well for you. Reinforce their behaviors with lavish praise—the easiest, fastest way to ensure others continue their non-distracting behaviors.

Here's an example used by a mother who runs a home-based business.

> *Karen, a speaker/coach, has nine-year-old twins—and she homeschools them. She coaches via telephone in late afternoons and evenings three times a week, and she attends to her presentations and business activities on the other two. Although she structures her time efficiently, she has a thorn in her side. Her oldest living relative, her favorite aunt, who is ill calls at all hours of the day and night. Although she feels empathetic about her aunt's loneliness and medical needs, Karen has to stop the calls during her work time. So she now tells her aunt, "It's great when you call right after lunch or dinner. The kids can say hello, and I'm able to give you my undivided attention. I appreciate it most when you call at those times."*

As Karen did, become mindful of how you can make positive comments. For example, reinforce positive behaviors by sending a note, e-mail, or special recognition. Bottom line: people respond best when they know what helpful actions to take.

Issues and Strategies: The Social Media Revolution

Have you noticed the revolution involving all ages of our population that fosters connection among individuals and groups across the globe? In fact, two-thirds of today's global Internet population, a staggering number, visits social networks. For example, it is said that Facebook has one billion users.

What do these statistics mean for you as a plugged-in adult? Not only are family, friends, and coworkers calling and e-mailing you, but you are actively connecting and communicating with people you may not even know. Have you noticed how building your own social network requires time, thus diverting your attention from other tasks? Some people check their social media sites so frequently that they fail to complete their professional work.

Don't allow the tentacles of technology-based social communication ensnare you. Take note of the actual time you waste. If you need to reduce it (highly likely):

- Impose an *electronic lockdown* during work time.

- Schedule appropriate times to participate.

- Alert your friends about your schedule change.

Issues and Strategies: Faulty Thinking as an Invitation to the *Others* Demon

Faulty thinking refers to a lack of clear thinking or logical conclusion. It includes harboring an erroneous assumption that leads to the wrong conclusion or oversimplifying an issue and exaggerating its possible effect. What emotions flood or overwhelm reason? Note these examples of faulty thinking:

- All-or-none thinking: "If I can't get two weeks of vacation, it's not worth taking."

- Now-or-never thinking: "If I don't get the promotion now, I never will."

- Discounting positives: "Even though I have a great performance appraisal, my ideas won't be accepted."

- Maximizing: "Unless I accept all phone calls or staff interruptions, I'm not a good boss."

- Minimizing: "When she calls me at work, we only talk for a minute." (Yeah, right!)

- Mind reading: "If I ask a question, my coworkers will think less of me."

How is faulty thinking related to distraction? When you hold unrealistic expectations and distorted perceptions, you lack balance and even feel overwhelmed or cornered. When you have more realistic expectations and flexibility, you feel a greater sense of control and peacefulness. More than that, you bypass the all-or-nothing, now-or-never attitude and increase the odds of acting on your own behalf.

When you're feeling calm and alert, allow time to review emotional situations from a logical perspective. Ask, "What's the big picture? Does anyone have malicious intentions? Did someone just make a mistake?" In this way, you separate your quick reactions from the facts. Also, tell others in a positive way what you need or want. This helps you reduce distraction, increase achievement, and attain greater satisfaction.

Review the tips below and check any that you're willing to try during the next week:

___ Deal with the specific problem of distraction, rather than the person. Instead of yelling, "You're so inconsiderate. Leave me alone!" say, "When developing a proposal, I work best when I have no interruptions. I need more quiet time."

___ Deal with the specific type of distraction and its effects on performance by saying, for example, "I lose my train of thought every time the phone rings." Then turn off the phone!

___ Say no, but say it nicely. For example, when someone says, "You have to hear this joke," say, "I'd love to, but I can't right now. I'm in the middle of something. When can we touch base?"

___ Don't overapologize or give excuses. Say, "I'm going to take my breaks away from my desk" rather than, "I'm taking my breaks away from my desk. I'm sorry if this is an inconvenience. I mean, I apologize, but I need to refresh and refuel. I must be tired, so excuse me."

___ Take ownership of a problem by saying something like, "When I'm balancing accounts, I attain better accuracy when it's quiet."

___ Allow time for decision making when another person makes a request instead of responding immediately. To buy more time, say, "Let me think it over and get back to you."

Issues and Strategies: Emotional Transitions

"Have it your way!" says Noreen's husband as he stomps out of the house. Still fuming over the argument, Noreen grabs her key ring and

purse, and she dashes to the car parked in the garage. Distracted by her emotions, Noreen backs into the side of the garage, smashing her car's back fender and taillight and scrapes the garage doorway.

Clearly, Noreen needed to calm down before she got behind the wheel. In this case, an emotional exchange distracted her, and the consequences were a high repair bill. She was lucky. What if a driver distracted by emotions runs into a cyclist or pedestrian, causing injury or death?

When you feel highly charged, you're vulnerable to other demons, such as the Technology Demon. As an example, a superintendent accidentally forwarded to one of her critics an e-mail in which she vented her frustrations about the school staff. That started a firestorm of controversy that turned her private annoyance into a highly public one.

When your emotions run high, take time to calm down. Period. Transition from that highly triggered state to one that allows for greater focus and vigilance. One instant of inattention can lead to a needless accident, resulting in financial distress as well as possible pain and suffering. Follow Thomas Jefferson's advice: "When angry, count to ten before you speak. If very angry, count to one hundred." In addition, you can listen to soft music, take a soothing bath, or breathe deeply several times. Many people feel that exercise reduces stress. See chapter 8 for other calming tips.

Issue and Strategies: Interruptions

According to personality-style inventories, some people love to be needed, liked, and accepted. Although they can be extremely competent in work situations or in social situations, their personality style and needs can result in a heightened vulnerability to others' interruptions. Here's an example.

Wade, a social worker, has fifteen years of experience working in a community-based mental health center. A great problem solver, he enjoys being friendly and helpful. In fact, he often stops to ask others if they need help. However, things seem to be getting out of hand; he's constantly interrupted by coworkers who contact him when they're facing difficulties. He's everyone's "go-to" guy. Given his additional paperwork and administrative duties, he's falling behind and staying overtime to finish his work. He knows he has to reduce the interruptions, yet he feels trapped because he doesn't want to be unkind.

Do you need to avoid or reduce the distractions imposed by others in your work/life? How can you protect yourself? Review this list, and check the tactics you're willing to try in the next week or two.

___ Post a message. "Business hours are from 9 A.M. to 7:30 P.M. Responses to e-mail, text, or other contacts received after business hours will be attended to within the next business day."

___ Hang a sign on the door. Do NOT DISTURB: GENIUS AT WORK. VISITORS WELCOME DURING BREAKS AT 11 A.M. AND 2 P.M.

___ Send a note or text message. "I am finishing my work. I'm not trying to upset or ignore you."

___ Leave a voice mail. "I'd like to participate in the project, but at this time, I'm unable to give it my all." Include in your voice mail the best times to call, the times during which you will return calls, and your e-mail address. This reduces telephone tag.

___ Reach out to others when you need information or help with a task. Don't distract yourself by worrying about what others will think of you. Usually, two heads are better than one—especially when dealing with difficult people or lacking clear directions.

___ List one or two ways to monitor and recognize others' efforts and maintain their motivation.

Once you understand the ways others distract and drain your mental energy, review the ways the Technology and the *Others* Demons can gang up to interfere with your performance at work, school, or home.

Issues and Strategies: Difficult (or Bullying) Interactions

The stress associated with tough economic times often leads to increases in negative interactions within families and among team members. Whether at home or at work, negative exchanges distract you and drain your energy. As you've probably observed, when you feel tired you have less energy, so your productivity drops.

Office bullying, including persistent, offensive, intimidating, or insulting behavior, poses a particularly difficult scenario. In some situations, you can deal with teasing, gossiping, or sabotaging behavior by ignoring it; in other situations, you're wise to be more direct. Take your time when deciding which approach to use. To gain perspective, talk to trusted coworkers, managers, friends, or family members. Once you decide on a good approach, then plan and prepare.

How many times have the constant interruptions of a coworker during a team meeting bothered you? Instead of telling off that person, use your logic and problem-solving skills to prepare a script (Bower and Bower, 2004.) That's what Elaine did. This office manager in a loud, busy insurance agency was puzzled about what to say to stop the bullying. Here's the script she prepared guided by five action steps.

1. **Visualize and describe the situation:** "We need uninterrupted time to work on these closings. You've been getting up to answer the phone even though we had scheduled this as *protected think time*."

2. **Write out the feelings and thoughts you want to express:** "I'm irritated, and I'm concerned that the project won't be finished on time or we will omit a critical detail or important aspect."

3. **Specify what you want:** "We need thirty minutes of quiet time to analyze the options and make decisions. Without *protected think time*, the team can't finish this project with the accuracy and completeness required."

4. **Talk about positive and/or negative consequences and specify a goal:** "The result of this project will be included in the annual report, so it needs to be accurate and complete. Let's work together so we can be proud of the result."

5. **Rehearse, perhaps with a friend or colleague:** "Practice makes perfect." That's the accepted advice for improving performance in the arts and sports. Often, though, when it comes to improving social skills, people ignore the idea of practice. If you're shy or fearful of others' reactions, you can improve your skills with practice. Plan, write notes, and schedule times to go over your script. Consider working with a colleague or friend and/or using an audio or video recording as a practice aid.

Prepare and practice positive assertive responses to the sticky situations you face. Consider the following questions.

- What can you say when your loved one becomes angry and says, "If you love me, you wouldn't tell me not to call to say hello during the day—even if you're working." You might respond positively by saying, "I love you and I need to focus on work. Let's touch base at lunch when I can pay full attention to you."

- What can you say when your coworker requests a minute to answer a question, but from past experience, you know that one minute is never fewer than ten or fifteen minutes? Some coworkers even ask, "You don't mind doing this extra job, do you?" You might respond positively by saying, "Good question. I think it requires a few minutes to answer it. Let's plan a time to deal with this properly," or "At this time, I'm swamped with other responsibilities. What are the alternatives?"

- What can you say when you need more quiet, *protected think time* to complete a project, but you fear that others will judge you as less than competent? You might respond positively by saying, "I do my best analytic thinking when it's quiet and I have no interruptions."

Issue and Strategies: Don't Let Distractions Undermine Your Friendships

On one hand, others can distract you from concentrating on important work tasks. On the other hand, situations at work (like a coworker having cancer) can distract you too. Are you the good friend you'd like to be? Do you follow through on your finest intentions? Do you call, send a card, or offer a ride?

However, when friends are in need, too often distractions provide an excuse for inaction. You don't know what to say; you don't want to intrude. The question is, how can you be supportive without getting swallowed up in the other person's whole experience? To ensure that another's difficulty doesn't become a total distraction for you, identify particular tasks you want to do and schedule times to follow through. At a minimum, call or write a note. Offer to walk the dog, prepare a meal, and/or take notes at an appointment. Perhaps you can assist in communicating with neighbors and coworkers about how they can contribute and be supportive. (To read amazingly heartfelt stories of support, go to the *Ladies' Home Journal* online at www.lhj.com/friendship.)

Issue and Strategies: Taking Care of the Caregiver

Caregivers feel responsible for a loved one and are at high risk for both mental and physical illness due to chronic stress, often unpredictable circumstances, and exhaustion (Schulz and Sherwood, 2008). While taking care of others, many people forget to take care of themselves. Bit by bit, they fall into a habit of:

- Devoting too many hours to the care of a person who's ill or elderly

- Ignoring the needs of other important people at work or home

Caregivers often brush off both good advice and dire warnings about the wear and tear brought on by their responsibilities. One or two sessions with a social worker or counselor can help the caregiver find better balance.

As her mother's health deteriorates, the amount of time, money, and energy Jill devotes to her parent's care increases. On the home front, her teenagers are taking advantage of her absences by having parties or coming home later than permitted. Jill has increasingly more headaches and sleepless nights. Her friend suggests keeping a journal to provide a forum for expressing her frustration. Journal writing serves to relieve her stress, but even more important, Jill reviews her journal entries and identifies critical issues she hadn't considered. As a result, she's aware that she needs help, and she contacts the geriatric center at a university medical center.

Increase your awareness of the situation by assessing it. That includes asking and answering the following questions:

- What is a reasonable amount of time to spend doing caregiving activities, given the health and safety factors of the person who needs care?

- What is a reasonable amount of time to spend, given your job, family, and other commitments?

- What resources are available to help with the details of personal care, finances, insurance, and health services?

- What limits might you impose to ensure a parent or loved one stays healthy and safe? For example, at what point should a parent stop driving or living alone?

- How well is the caregiver taking care of the health and well-being of other family members?

- How well is the caregiver taking care of himself or herself?

- To what degree are family members included in the problem-solving and decision-making processes?

- How are caregiving duties distracting the caregiver from other critical responsibilities?

Writing about and assessing the situation puts you in a better position to gain advice from such experts or support groups as Caregivers Survival Institute (info@ caregivingburnout.org). When you put your thoughts on paper, you tend to be less distracted by them.

Use Demon-Defying Strategies

Yes, you need an arsenal of ways to establish new behaviors that will reduce distractions from others. Often, you find power in numbers. Using several strategies in sequence or in combination provides the power needed to take on the *Others* Demon. You might begin by engaging in visualization and self-dialogue to heighten your awareness and boost your motivation. Review the following list of strategies, and check those that might help you during the next week.

___ *Use visualization.* Imagine ways that others can help you even more than they are.

___ *Use reason.* If you want to enhance your productivity (and decrease your stress), it's necessary to take action against the distractions imposed by others at work or home. Become mindful of the time and energy the *Others* Demon wastes. Is it worth your effort to stop some of the distractions some of the time?

___ *Use constructive self-talk.* Talk or write about the wonderful ways you're productive when you have undisturbed quiet, quality work time. Refer to a reminder like, "I'm in control of most of the conditions around me. I can improve the quality, accuracy, and completeness of my work if I create more positive conditions."

___ *Use positive assertiveness.* Share articles to initiate a conversation about the effect of interruptions on work productivity and quality. Use information you've gleaned to discuss the need for fewer interruptions among team members.

___ *Set productive routines.* Identify "No Interruption Time" periods. Make a team effort to protect think time and reduce distractions four times a week for twenty to thirty minutes each.

___ *Use the Stop, Look, and Listen technique.* When you feel overwhelmed or on the spot, simply stop, look, listen. Stop: Refrain from action for a minute or two. Look: Imagine the difficulties encountered and ways you or others have solved them. Listen: Activate your inner voice, repeat the lessons you've learned, and take action.

___ *Seek social support.* When it comes to communication and potential conflict with others, seek the support and insights of a friend, colleague, or person with special training. Fear of conflict and humiliation can eat away your intentions to take action against the *Others* Demon—even when warranted!

Moving from Intention to Action

Over time, constant distraction by others can increase stress, forgetfulness, and disorganization. All of this decreases your effectiveness. How can you make headway against others who derail you at work or at home?

Start by answering the questions listed with each step. They will guide you from good intention to positive action:

1. *Assess.* Visualize work/life activities in which your productivity suffers due to distractions and interruptions. Ask, "How is the *Others* Demon interfering with my productivity?" Write down what you specifically want certain people to stop or start doing.

_____

_____

_____

2. *Analyze consequences.* List the costs and benefits of others' distractions as they relate to your work/life activities. Estimate the time, money, and energy you waste due to distractions. Ask, "As I try to complete my daily activities, to what degree are distractions from others affecting my productivity and wasting time or money?" Decide if the effort to change is worthwhile.

_____

_____

_____

3. *Set realistic goals.* Visualize ways to move toward more positive consequences. Ask, "What are one or two goals I can set to decrease the distractions imposed by others and increase my performance?" Remember, it takes conscious effort to resist the distractions posed by others, and it's always difficult. Today's conditions make the task even more challenging. So start small, but start. Here's a sample goal to consider:

Goal: To have twenty to forty minutes each day (or each week) free from the interruptions of others. Write down what you will *say* or *do* to ensure your *protected think time.*

- At work: _____

- At home: _____

- Other settings: _____

4. *Take action.* Identify strategies to remove or decrease distractions imposed by others. Refer to the list of Demon-Defying Strategies and ask, "When, where, and how will I move from intention to action?" and "What specific strategies or tips will I use?"

_____

_____

_____

5. *Monitor and maintain progress.* The more frequently you reward your efforts to stop others from imposing distractions, the more easily you'll keep going in the right direction. Ask, "How will I track progress toward my goal? What rewards or incentives can I access to sustain motivation? How can I deal with barriers or other demons? What resources or experts might I contact if I have questions or need support?"

_____

_____

_____

A checklist helps you maintain your efforts or alter them (or both). Here's a sample checklist that can keep you on track. Be sure to monitor your progress and congratulate yourself at various stages as you battle the *Others* Demon.

Monitoring Actions Against the Others Demon

	Work	Home	Other
Limit social networking.			
Let others know what you need.			

Compliment others who do not interrupt.			
Take time for emotional transitions.			
Put up a sign, and schedule a time to inform others about your work times.			
Practice nicely saying no to unacceptable requests.			

Tony's *Others* Success Story

Tony is a work-at-home dad. His extremely homesick college freshman calls him three or four times a day. Tony has two goals. He wants to be there for his son, and he wants to earn enough money to keep his son in school. After numerous conversations about alternatives for his son's well-being, Tony realizes he needs to impose a rule and establish a routine. Speaking to his son, he says, "I want to know about what's going on, so I want to talk to you when I'm best able to listen. You know, business is down, and the only way to boost sales is to make more cold calls. I'd like to schedule our phone conversations before and after the times I need to concentrate and make lots of cold calls. Let's try that for a week or so and see how it goes."

Do you see how Tony uses positive assertiveness and a productive routine to reduce distractions imposed by his son? You can too!

THE ACTIVITIES DEMON

The Activities Demon attacks us when we inappropriately multi task, travel, rush, or face tedious, difficult tasks. The emotionality of events like holidays makes us easy prey for distractions.

Actions Against the Activities Demon

Lu Chen is a charming sales representative for a tractor company. A winner of major awards for his promotions and sales, he easily develops relationships with customers and vendors alike. However, he is lackadaisical when it comes to administrative tasks. He complains, "Those tedious tasks take time away from my sales promotions." Consequently, he puts them off and then rushes to complete them by the deadline, and he inevitably makes mistakes. His error rate swiftly soars when he overuses multitasking. For example, while on the telephone, he scratches notes on envelopes, sticks receipts in pockets, or tucks memos into the wrong files.

Lu is highly susceptible to the distractions posed by the Activities Demon. First, he needs to complete numerous activities that he doesn't like and isn't good at. Second, distracted by social interactions in his area of strength, he procrastinates when faced with tedious recordkeeping, an activity in his area of greatest vulnerability. Lastly, he has multitask-itis; he overuses his ability to do several activities simultaneously. He inadvertently makes more work for himself because of his mistakes.

Know that the type of activity you engage in directly affects your ability to sustain your attention. If you want to increase performance and productivity, examine the most common activities you're required to do and identify the ones that distract you the most. Then ask these questions:

- How much difficulty do I have when I try to complete activities that are boring or tedious?

- Do I ignore tasks involving finances, legal matters, health, travel, or home maintenance?

- Which activities most trigger distractions and lead to my ineffectiveness?

This chapter can help you work through those questions. It provides charts, checklists, and tips for your Plan of Attack against the distractions you confront at work, at home, or during travel. The important issues addressed include multitasking, finances, transitions, and procrastination.

Attack of the Activities Demon

Americans are constantly busy with a wide variety of activities. Too many people, however, perceive that they don't get anything done. Although they're busier than ever, they're plagued with feeling scattered and unfulfilled.

How have average citizens been using their time (in what activities)? The federal government provides the following statistics for 2009 (US Bureau of Labor Statistics, 2010):

- Work activities. Employed persons worked an average of seven and one half hours on the days they worked.

- Household activities. On an average day, 85 percent of women and 67 percent of men spent time doing household activities (housework, cooking, lawn and car maintenance, or financial and other household management tasks). Women spent more than two and one-half hours on such activities, while men spent two hours.

- Leisure activities. On an average day, nearly everyone fifteen and over engaged in some sort of leisure activity, such as watching TV, socializing, or exercising. Men spent more time (5.8 hours) than women did (5.1 hours) on these activities. Adolescents between fifteen and nineteen years old read for an average of five minutes per weekend day; they spent one hour playing games or using a computer for leisure. (The Technology Demon at work.)

- Care of household children (for the period 2005 to 2009). Adults living in households with children under six spent an average of two hours per day providing primary childcare to household children. The amount of time spent in these activities for children between the years six and seventeen was less than half that time—forty-seven minutes per day.

Many of the activities included in the nine and one-half or ten hours devoted to work and household activities might be mundane. But this is exactly the time you're most vulnerable to distraction, disorganization, and stress.

The Activities Demon attacks when you're facing activities you consider difficult, boring, or irrelevant—whether at work, home, or during travel. This demon makes it difficult to begin a task, stop your mind from wandering, attend to and recall detail, and take time to organize. You might be especially vulnerable to distraction when you lack clear directions or are working toward deadlines far into the future. Perhaps you procrastinate or push toward perfectionism. Consequently, you can lose sight of the big picture and spin your wheels.

However, once you know the types of activities that trigger distraction and procrastination, you can create a Plan of Attack to confront the Activity Demon. The following self-check helps you to do that.

Self-Check: The Activities Demon

Directions: Read each statement and place a check beside all statements that apply to you.

_____ 1. I avoid responsibilities for which I lack interest or skill.

_____ 2. I make careless mistakes when working on tedious tasks.

_____ 3. I over-schedule and can't concentrate on getting one thing done at a time.

_____ 4. I don't task enough questions about activities when I'm unsure of directions or standards.

_____ 5. I'm in "multitask mode" too often and experience slippages in my performance.

_____ 6. I'm forgetful, especially when I'm overscheduled.

_____ 7. I'm especially disorganized when I'm engaged in particular activities such as:

_____

If you checked more than a few statements, you're particularly vulnerable to the Activities Demon. You may benefit from slowing down and taking more frequent brief breaks.

General Consequences of the Activities Demon

Hundreds of years ago, during Queen Victoria's reign, Lord Alfred Tennyson, England's poet laureate, said, "So much to do, so little done, such things to be."

This is the lament of many in the workforce who can't seem to balance all of their overflowing work/life activities. Constantly juggling activities and schedules, they feel overwhelmed, stressed, fatigued, unproductive—and never satisfied. Business and industry attempt to reduce the debilitating effect of this constant overwhelm. They provide work/life balance strategies like flex time, on-site gyms, and child-care services—solutions that are linked to less absenteeism and more productivity.

At first glance, it appears the problem involves poor time management, but in reality, it relates to task management. The question becomes how many activities are enough—both for individuals and for society?

Are you aware of ways you can appropriately delegate within the limits of your role and responsibility? Can you simplify schedules and focus on those tasks that have the highest priority? Certainly, the distractions that various activities pose can detract from your ability to "get things done." Several strategies follow.

Assess: Keep a Weekly Calendar

Do these phrases sound familiar to you? "I'm rushing from one thing to another. I never seem to have enough time. I'm exhausted by three in the afternoon." What activities are you shoving into your schedule? Do you have any breaks? Do you allow enough time to comfortably get where you're going?

It's time to gain information about your own state of constant overwhelm and how your activities contribute to feeling disorganized or dissatisfied. Use the following schedule to track your activities for one week. Color-code different activities, such as work or personal, etc., to track them more easily.

Weekly Calendar

Hours	Sunday	Monday	Tuesday	Wednesday	Thursday	Friday	Saturday
6 a.m.							
7 a.m.							
8 a.m.							
9 a.m.							
10 a.m.							
11 a.m.							
12 p.m.							
1 p.m.							
2 p.m.							
3 p.m.							
4 p.m.							
5 p.m.							
6 p.m.							
7 p.m.							
8 p.m.							
9 p.m.							
10 p.m.							
11 p.m.							
12 a.m.							
1 a.m.							

Identify the times you're most likely to feel "productive and satisfied" versus "rushed or overwhelmed." Do you allow enough time between appointments, or are you often late to meetings?

When you become more conscious of your activities and how they contribute to distraction, you're more prepared to improve productivity and reduce stress. To become more aware, ask and answer these questions:

- When, where, and how are various activities having a negative effect on my attention, organization, memory, or mood?

- What am I doing currently to improve my organization so I can be more productive?

- When rushed or overwhelmed, do I tend to engage in such self-defeating behaviors as over- or under-eating or excessive smoking, drinking, or procrastination?

Analyze Personal Consequences

What types of activities distract you from completing the important tasks you're responsible for? Ask this question when you feel like you're spinning your wheels or are forgetful and disorganized.

It's said that 80 percent of your productivity results from 20 percent of your effort. As you visualize your workday, ask, "Which activities, conditions, and consequences account for 80 percent of my accomplishments?" List these activities, and give them the highest priority. Schedule them when you anticipate having the fewest distractions.

In the chart, list any negative health, performance, or social consequences you experience as a result of the Activities Demon. Then rate the degree of negativity, using a scale from one to ten, with ten being the highest degree.

Identifying Negative Consequences of the Activities Demon

Situations in Which the Activities Demon Interferes with Productivity	Negative Health Consequences	Negative Productivity Consequences	Negative Social Consequences
1.			
2.			
3.			

Can you think of *positive* consequences? If so, note them here.

_____

_____

Be mindful of how different activities or tasks trigger distractions by addressing such questions as:

- Which activities or tasks tend to trigger distraction for me?

  _____

- When, where, and how is the activity having a negative effect on my attention?

  _____

- What am I doing to manage the activities and tasks I'm responsible for? In what ways are my solutions working?

  _____

- How do I feel about these situations?

  _____

- What benefits might I gain from outsourcing or delegating routine or administrative tasks?

  _____

Set Realistic Goals to Manage the Activities Demon

Commonly, you may underestimate the time required to complete an activity while over-estimating your skills or the resources you need. Work backward: from a vision of the outcome, next visualize the beginning and middle phases. Ask, "What steps must be followed to complete this activity?"

- Such thinking leads to developing doable goals. You create a series of steps; your stress decreases; your motivation and attention increase. For example, your general goals might be:

- Schedule activities that require accuracy and detail when I'm most alert and least distracted. This might include reading financial, legal, or tax reports.

- Take breaks when doing difficult or tedious tasks, especially when working in my areas of vulnerability.

To make these goals more doable, identify one activity to do once a week (or once a month) at a particular time of day. Visualize or review your schedule to identify a small, simple goal to reduce the vulnerability posed by the Activities Demon. What could you say or do to ensure you have non-distracted productivity time?

- At work _____

- At home _____

- Other setting _____

Major Strategy: Scheduling

If it's worth doing at all, it's worth writing down and scheduling. That's your first resolve. Also avoid falling into the *death-by-sticky-note* syndrome. If you need to write a note, take a few seconds to tack it to a bulletin board or record it in your PDA, phone, or notebook. Don't let those sticky notes disappear!

When making a list, limit the number of tasks you put on it, and separate the items into short- and long-term goals. You can brainstorm about things you eventually want to do and create a bigger list, but remember, list making is only the first step of your Plan of Attack. Too often, people become so overwhelmed with long lists of items, they fail to prioritize and schedule. Sometimes, several short lists keep you going better. They present a "divide-and-conquer" strategy that breaks the action items into *doable* parts.

Follow this five-step process faithfully:

1. List the things you want to accomplish and categorize each under three headings: Urgent, Necessary, or Nice.

2. Visualize ways to implement each activity or task.

3. Estimate or *guesstimate* a range of time needed to complete the task; schedule that block of time on your calendar.

4. Engage in constructive self-talk while you schedule the tasks. As you move into the *real-time* world. Ask, "Are there too many items on my list? Do I need to prioritize, consolidate, and rearrange? In the past, how long have such tasks taken to complete?"

5. Check off each task as it's completed. If you can't finish one, note the reason, and add a suggestion to adjust what you did as a way to improve.

This process helps you use your logic, focus on tasks, set priorities and timelines, and, when necessary, provide information about adjustments to make. Because the best-laid plans go awry when interruptions occur, identify ways to set up the conditions necessary to complete the task. It causes you to slow down and tap into your logic to determine "what, when, and where" so you can complete your activities.

Sometimes feeling stressed about big-picture issues hinders your efforts to complete an activity. It's rarely about what to do; rather, it's where to start and what steps to take. Adapt steps and strategies according to your personal situation. Often, it helps to list the steps for the actual process you'll follow. This enables you to break the task into more manageable chunks.

Here's an example of the steps used by a landscape designer to plan and implement a design.

Carolyn's Steps to Complete Garden Designs

Step 1. To get the big picture, sketch the design for a client, including various beds and areas.

Step 2. Create a to-do list of different tasks to complete. For example, include what is necessary to purchase, prune, or mulch. Further define smaller tasks under each major task.

Step 3. Prioritize the to-do list and engage in problem solving. For example, ask, "If I need to prune, which area should be done first? Should some tasks be done in stages? Approximately how long might each task take?" Visualize what you need to do. Think, talk it out, and then write answers to your questions. Include the resources you need to access. This makes your plan a complete action guide because it includes what you need to do, phone numbers of resources, and expected completion time.

Step 4. Schedule the tasks on a calendar. To save time, you can insert the phone numbers within the time slots to locate them easily. Once you schedule tasks on a calendar, you may see ways of accomplishing tasks within chunks of time. For example, if you need to do research for two clients simultaneously, list times when you can complete similar tasks for both clients.

Step 5. Schedule five to ten minutes each night to check off the tasks you completed during the day and list those you need to complete the next day.

Issues and Strategies: The Myth and Madness of Multitasking

More mess results from multitasking than meets the eye. For example, while Lu, the sales representative, is attempting to do two or three things at once, he's also spilling soda on piled file folders, misplacing forms, and, as the day progresses, feeling increasingly fatigued, forgetful, and irritable. As he stresses out about late reports, inaccurate orders, and numerous slipups, Lu realizes the frequent mishaps that occur while multitasking cost him far more than he imagined. Lu bought into the myth that multitasking saves time, but he realizes that in the end, multitasking wastes precious time and energy.

Throughout society, inappropriate multitasking—especially when using technology—constitutes madness. The headline CALIFORNIA BANS TEXTING BY OPERATORS OF TRAINS (McKinley and Wald, 2008) illustrates this point. Who doesn't accept the fact that certain activities, like operating a train, require total, uninterrupted attention? When activities involve human health and safety, multitasking should never be tolerated. In this particular situation, the engineer was sending and receiving text messages when he ran a red light near Los Angeles. In the resulting crash, 25 people were killed and 130 injured—the worst train accident in the United States since 1993.

Sometimes multitasking involves a mundane act such as drinking coffee that can still have potentially costly and dangerous consequences. Recently, a pilot spilled his coffee on the control panel and triggered a hijacking alert (Gillies, 2011). The Boeing 777 carrying 241 passengers and 14 crewmembers made an unscheduled stop. How much stress, fear, and expense did that avoidable mishap involve?

For most, multitasking isn't catastrophic, but its effects sap their energy and drag down their productivity. When workers attempt to do two things quickly and simultaneously, inaccuracies and omissions abound. According to Dr. Edward Hallowell, "Multitasking creates the illusion that we're getting more done, but we really can't pay simultaneous attention to two demanding tasks. It diminishes the quality of work on both" (Crawford, 2009). In addition, studies indicate that we lose time and increase stress by constantly switching tasks, even when the switch only takes a few seconds. In fact, research reveals that those who multitask the most are those who are worst at it (*Stanford News*, 2009). The simplest strategy is to think about what you're doing and elect to do tasks at a slower pace, one at a time.

Are you pushing yourself to do too many things at one time? This checklist will help you answer that question.

Self-Check: Multitasking Activities

Directions: Read each item and check all that apply to you.

___ 1. The amount of multitasking I do at work is increasing.

___ 2. I think that my performance at work suffers due to multitasking.

___ 3. I think that my performance at home suffers due to multitasking.

___ 4. Although I know that multitasking is ineffective, I still do it frequently.

___ 5. I seem less organized when I multitask.

Consider setting aside times when you can concentrate on one task at a time—without thinking about other activities you need to do. Remember, especially when analytical thinking is required, stop multitasking. Do one thing at a time.

Issues and Strategies: Travel

Even the super-organized become frazzled when traveling, especially when they don't follow their established routines. That's when they become more vulnerable to distraction, forgetfulness, and disorganization. One ordinarily savvy traveler tells the following story (Rand, 2010) that teaches an important lesson.

> *Greg Rand, a managing partner at a realty company, relates a nightmare travel experience. Greg prides himself on being a super-organized traveler. Not only does he have his own routines for check-in and security, he preaches to his wife about the routines she should follow. Typically, he hires a car service to get to the airport. On this one trip, however, he drives his wife's car to New York's LaGuardia Airport. At the curbside check-in, an agent distracts him when requesting that he enter the terminal. It's only when he's on the plane and thinking about his smooth arrival that he can't remember how he parked the car. Oops! He didn't park the car; he left it idling curbside. Coming back several days later, he makes a mad dash for the impound lot, pays $200, and retrieves his wife's car—luckily undamaged.*

This example highlights the fact that no one is exempt from the distractions inherent in travel activities. You need established routines to protect yourself from mishaps, but understand that, even with precautions, slipups can occur before, during, and after departure.

To avoid mistakes, ask, "How can I keep on track without misplacing or forgetting items when I travel?" Use the following list (or create your own) of items to take when traveling or working on the road. Tape your list where you'll see it, and check it as you depart.

Checklist: What Do You Need?

___ Room key and hotel information, such as room number, address, map, fax or phone number

___ Daily schedule, addresses, phone numbers, directions for appointments

___ Keys to car or change to pay for transportation

___ Wallet, cash, credit cards

___ PDA or cell phone

___ Client records, presentation materials

___ Paper and pen

___ Water and snack

___ Umbrella, plastic jacket, and/or sweater

___ Prescriptions and over-the-counter medications, such as antacids or allergy pills

You can create lists for winter or summer travel or, like a sales rep named Roberto does, make charts describing the clothes to pack and the logistics you'll need to consider.

When you return from a vacation or business trip, take time to put things away, and prepare to resume your regular work/life activities. This checklist facilitates the transition from travel back to work.

Checklist: Returning from Vacation or a Business Trip

___ 1. Put laundry and/or cleaning in appropriate places.

___ 2. Unpack suitcase.

___ 3. Sort, file, or discard papers, bills, receipts, souvenirs, and business cards.

___ 4. Replenish sundries and store in travel bag for next trip.

___ 5. Put away books, articles, and newly acquired materials.

___ 6. Schedule times for follow-up calls, e-mails, and other correspondence.

Keeping a travel journal can help. Perhaps you enjoy an annual fishing or camping trip. Don't get distracted when you get home and fail to note the changes you'll need to make for the next year. Take a small notebook so you can jot down notes about unexpected problems or extra items to bring. If a journal doesn't suit your style, a simple pre-packing list could suffice. Or you might store all special items for your trip in a separate suitcase, duffle, or carton.

Right after you return home, refill your basic supplies so they're ready for the next trip. For example, Damon, a single parent, goes to a family camp each summer. As soon as he finishes the laundry, he puts the camp towels in duffle bags right away so they're ready to take on the next trip. He replenishes, checks off, and repacks such supplies as sunscreen, aspirin, batteries, plastic baggies, and other sundries.

It sounds simple, but it took three years of running around the night before camp to convince Damon of the value of planning and preparation. He also uses visualization to plan. For example, he flashed back to his kindergartner's crying jag because he forgot the extra batteries for the flashlight on the last trip. "Okay, this time I pack batteries," he tells himself.

Unfortunately, in a hurried, harried, and security-driven society, travel can mean multiplied hassles. There's only one antidote: Plan for the rigors and distractions.

Issues and Strategies: Special Occasions and Holidays

You don't have to be a wedding maven to realize the myriad details screaming for attention when planning a large event. The pressure peaks on the big day, when everyone is expected to arrive on time. One wedding guest tells this story about the morning of the nuptials.

> *The bride, her parents, and the bridesmaids pile into a limousine and head for the church, with other guests and family members arriving on their own. As the jittery wedding party heads into town, the driver slows down at a stoplight next to a bus stop. It takes a moment for the bride to realize that the carefully attired elderly woman waiting for the bus is her eighty-something-year-old great aunt! In the chaos of arranging rides for the many out-of-town relatives, no one remembered to pick up Aunt Georgia. Hastily, the driver assists Aunt Georgia into the packed limo. An independent sort, she laughs as she nestles next to the bride and quips, "What's the big deal? I always take the bus."*

Remember the adage, "Rome wasn't built in a day"? When you break tasks into small steps, you allow for the time needed to focus, plan, and organize activities. Whether preparing for a special occasion or a holiday, when you identify a few tasks to complete each day, week, or month, it's easy to remain motivated and on target.

Regardless of your level of competence and motivation, special occasions do breed distractions. When you're overloaded, stressed, and perhaps fatigued, you can face several demons—the Stress Demon, the Fatigue Demon, and the Unruly-Mind Demon—at once.

On this list, check any suggestions you might consider as special occasions rotate through the year:

___ Consider the budget and any financial constraints.

___ Brainstorm all the activities to be completed.

___ Organize the activities by category (e.g., invitations, locations, events, etc.).

___ Note the event on a calendar and work backward to heed various deadlines. For example, if the invitations must be in the mail midmonth, by when must you deliver the artwork to the printer?

___ Delegate jobs whenever possible, but provide instructions and models for the tasks you want others to do.

___ Keep up-to-date records and organized and handy receipts in an accordion folder.

___ Plan additional formal meetings with those involved with the event.

Issues and Strategies: Finance

It's easy to allow distractions to interfere with completing critical but tedious activities related to taxes, finances, legal issues, or health matters. Whether routine or occasional, you suffer significant negative consequences when these activities are delayed, incomplete, or inaccurate.

Distractions can drastically affect your cash flow and money management, as these examples show.

- *An unexpected, one-time-only incident:* When purchasing a new king-size mattress, Vince thinks it's a great idea to accept the furniture company's "No Interest for Two Years!" offer. He mails each monthly payment on time but then loses track of the due date for the last payment. Late with the final payment, he then receives an invoice for all of the past interest, compounded—a large expense. He stews about it for ages.

- Expected, ongoing responsibilities: Theresa, an independent sales consultant for a costume jewelry line, sends invoices and collects payments with efficiency.

However, chaos reigns when it comes to her personal financial records. In some years, late fees and penalties to the IRS or credit card companies eat up the extra money she makes from her sales. She's frustrated about all her wasted effort.

Like Vince, you might experience late credit card or tax payments or home, car, or computer maintenance that results in fines, penalties, or unnecessarily large repair bills. Perhaps, like Theresa, you'd benefit from analyzing the consequences, setting a goal to avert problems, and taking action. Theresa figures she could have taken a nice vacation with the money she's wasted. She realizes if she doesn't schedule the task on a calendar, she won't complete it. So she resolves to use her calendar to schedule the necessary time—even thirty minutes a month—to file and organize her tax receipts.

On a national level, credit card companies impose arbitrary interest rate increases, so read the fine print about rates. Many companies state they have the right to change a rate at any time, for any reason. Becoming mindful of this possibility leads to better strategies for planning and execution. For some, having a simple visual reminder is helpful. If that's true for you, post a calendar in an accessible, visible place. Note dates on that calendar when important payments are due (e.g., insurance, rents, taxes, subscriptions, services, or licenses). Take thirty minutes to write all the dates on a calendar at the beginning of each quarter or at the beginning of each year. For some, an auditory reminder is best. You can program most computers and PDAs to alert you about upcoming tasks.

Don't forget to schedule a time to shred unwanted financial or legal papers. This helps avoid identity theft and hundreds of wasted dollars and hours of energy trying to resolve related issues.

Issues and Strategies: Procrastination

Everyone puts off the start of certain activities some of the time, but don't make procrastination a lifestyle. Why procrastinate? Sometimes it's because tasks are tedious, difficult, or time consuming. Other times, it's because you lack specific knowledge or skills, or you worry that you'll fail and look bad. Still other times, you can't make a decision, have unrealistic expectations, or are overwhelmed by the amount of effort required. Do you notice your psychic energy and creativity diminish when your thoughts are filled with phrases such as "I must" or "I ought to"?

When you allow a gift certificate to expire or a deadline to be missed, procrastination is at play. It can create tension and stress, especially if you disappoint others who depend on you.

In most cases, procrastination is a bad habit that you can alter. Check all of the following suggestions you'd use to cut down on your "I'll do it later" tendency.

___ List the specific tasks that trigger procrastination.

___ Identify both the external and internal consequences of putting them off.

___ Visualize the successful accomplishment of each task and say, "I need to do one step at a time" or "I'll finish the draft and see if I need more information."

___ Break complicated or long-term projects into easy-to-complete chunks, identifying mini-goals along the way.

___ Work toward each goal for brief periods, even as few as ten minutes at a time.

___ Make a game or challenge out of the task. Ask, "Can I complete one or two steps before the timer rings?"

___ Post a calendar that lists specific times to work on each chunk.

___ Collaborate with others to get each task started and completed.

___ Combat myths such as these: "I do my best under pressure; I need to complete the entire task in one sitting; I need more information or resources."

Issues and Strategies: Transitions

You rush home to start dinner. Then you drop a jar and spill a drink—you can't believe you are so inept. What's going on? In such cases, you fail to make a smooth transition from one activity to the next. Especially if you feel tired, rushed, or stressed, you need time to move from high gear to neutral and then warm up for the next activity.

No athlete or musician begins an event without taking time to warm up. If you experience small mishaps when you need to begin a task, then provide a few minutes for transitions. Try it. For the next few days, when planning appointments, chores, or meetings, schedule at least five to ten minutes of transition time between ending one task and beginning another—for your own sanity.

> *Rhonda works part-time as a CPA. She feels frazzled and stressed when she returns at the end of the day to her three children, ages five to twelve. The period between 5:00 and 9:00 p.m. is especially hectic; she feels distracted dealing with mealtime, homework, and bedtime routines. She employs a few simple strategies to maintain her energy and reduce the distractions that plague her. Rhonda combines visualization, constructive self-talk, and positive assertiveness with the Stop, Look, and Listen technique.*

It's your turn. Take a few minutes to review the following strategies. Check those activities you might try next week to improve transitioning between activities in your life.

___ Allot three to five minutes to breathe, visualize positive things, and relax before entering your house.

___ Take a minute or two to list various activities, and estimate the amount of time to allot to each. This avoids the 8:30 p.m. wail, "Mom, I forgot that I'm supposed to bring cupcakes to school tomorrow."

___ Include the children in a Stop, Look, and Listen technique in order to transition from care by the babysitter to care by the parent.

___ Use a timer to track your schedule of activities, including homework and bath time.

___ Create the family version of an *electronic lockdown*—a time of relaxation and recreation without television, phone calls, or computers. Consider creating a fun zone—a separate, protected space for playing with games and puzzles or reading books.

___ Be assertive. Alert family and friends that they'll receive calls, e-mails, and texts only after family time is over.

When you allow time for transitions and create routines to relax between events, you increase your ability to focus and achieve.

Issues and Strategies: Instructions and Assertiveness

The Activities Demon attacks when you feel unsure about what to do or how well to do it. If you lack clear instructions and standards, your attention wanders and you procrastinate or make mistakes. Too frequently, the resulting work is late, inaccurate, and/or incomplete.

Whether you're at work or home, make sure you have a full explanation of the tasks for which you're responsible. It's your right! Unfortunately, it's common to begin tasks without having the details necessary to get the job done. For example, when a nursing student asks about a master's thesis requirements, her instructor responds, "You'll know when you're finished." Under such circumstances, the instructor might respond negatively to the completed job and say, "That's not what I wanted" or "You didn't finish." Without asking questions assertively upfront, students—and employees—become extremely vulnerable to undue criticism. The result? Motivation wanes, productivity lags, and dissatisfaction prevails.

Your level of uncertainty rises when you lack clear directions, including specific standards, timelines, and possible resources. The greater your uncertainty about the activity, the greater the risk of unfulfilled expectations, inaccurate or incomplete tasks, and unnecessary stress.

Being assertive allows you to gain needed information to complete an activity successfully. Make sure you ask questions to clarify exactly what needs to be done and by when. It's common to feel unsure of what to say or to be afraid to look dumb. Consider these examples of what you might say in various situations.

- *If you lack clear directions*, say, "Let's clarify the goal and list the steps that need to be taken. This will ensure that things go as we need them to."

- *If you lack specific standards*, ask, "What questions need to be addressed in this report to make sure it's accurate, assuming that accuracy is the critical element in this project?"

- *If you lack a timetable or schedule*, ask, "Realistically, when would you like to receive this?"

- *If you lack knowledge about possible resources*, say, "If questions arise, who can I call? What resources are available?"

Whether the activity is assigned or self-imposed, clearly identify the tasks to do, when to do them, and how well to do them. Be assertive in asking questions of those who assign tasks.

Visualize a work/life situation in which you lack the information or resources you need to efficiently complete an activity. For one or two situations, describe ways you can get what you need by using positive assertiveness.

Situation 1: _____

Situation 2: _____

Assertive skills keep you on track and avoid the distractions presented by extra commitments and activities. When asked to take on a new volunteer job, for example, you might say, "I promised my family I wouldn't accept any new community commitments this year. Although I'm supportive of the cause, I'm unable to help at this time. Keep me on the list for another time."

Although taking on nonessential tasks is part of your community life, say no if volunteer work seriously distracts you from your work or home duties. When you receive extra requests for your time and energy, take the opportunity to say no nicely but firmly.

Use Demon-Defying Strategies

Imagine you have a large, cumbersome project that's due in several months. Before, you've tended to become overwhelmed and worried about its reception or evaluation. Typically, you procrastinate and then rush to complete such a project.

This time, review the following list of strategies, and check those that might help you during the next week.

___ *Use visualization.* Imagine the completed task. Then imagine the midpoint from completion. Once the task has a midpoint, it becomes easier to divide the task into small, easy-to-complete chunks.

___ *Use reason.* Visualize the negative effects of starting late, forgetting to plan or schedule your activities, and not completing activities for which you're responsible. Stop the stress response by taking deep breaths, thinking about your strengths, and visualizing your past successes. Imagine the positive feeling of doing one small task well. Isn't that likely to spur you on to do more?

___ *Use constructive self-talk.* Ask, "Are there any natural dividing lines? How long should this or that take under the best conditions? How long under the worst conditions?"

___ *Use positive assertiveness.* Identify and use your strengths. If you're asked to complete tasks in your areas of vulnerability, request more time, assistance, and resources. Discuss options if you know you can't do an assigned task because you lack the knowledge or skill. For example, say, "I'm a word person, so I'll be the note-taker. Let's find a designer to do the graphics."

___ *Institute productive routines.* Identify your high-energy times. If you're a morning person, then get up thirty to forty-five minutes earlier once a week so you can work on an important aspect of the project. Do the mundane tasks during low-energy times. Play lively music or use an appealing air freshener to boost your energy.

___ *Use the Stop, Look, and Listen technique.* When you feel overwhelmed or put on the spot, do this: Stop: refrain from action for a minute or two. Look: examine the conditions and consequences of the activity in your mind's eye. Imagine any difficulties you could encounter as you begin to work on the task. Listen: engage in self-dialogue that identifies the costs and benefits of the activity.

___ *Access social support.* Team up with a colleague or supervisor and use a checklist for planning arduous tasks. It provides a vehicle for conversation. You'll likely find that two heads make the time go faster, and together you might identify issues or roadblocks you hadn't considered before.

Moving from Intention to Action

Answer the following questions to guide you from good intention to positive action.

1. *Assess*. Visualize several work/life activities in which your productivity lags due to distractions, lack of adequate instructions, or tedium. Ask, "How is the Activity Demon interfering with my productivity?"

_____

_____

2. *Analyze consequences*. List the costs and consequences of distractions caused by particular activities within your work/life. Estimate the time, money, or energy you waste due to such distractions. Ask, "As I work to complete my daily tasks, to what degree is distraction interfering with my productivity, diminishing my image, or wasting my time or money?"

_____

_____

3. *Set realistic goals*: Visualize ways to help you move toward more positive consequences. Ask, "What one or two goals might decrease distractions and increase my performance when I'm engaged in important work/life activities?"

_____

_____

4. *Take action*. Note strategies you can take to remove or decrease distractions at work or home. Ask, "When, where, and how will I move from intention to action? What specific strategies or tips will I use?"

_____

_____

5. *Monitor and maintain progress*. The more frequently you reward and recognize your efforts to stop a distracting behavior like multitasking, the easier it is to keep going in the right direction. Ask, "How will I track my progress toward my goal? What rewards or incentives can I access to sustain motivation? How can I deal with

barriers or other demons? What resources or experts might I contact if I have questions or need support?"

_____

_____

Often, a checklist helps form a productive habit, especially when you're rushed or tired. Here's an example of a checklist to help you stay on track.

Monitoring Actions Against the Activities Demon

	At Work	At Home	Other Setting
Stop inappropriate multitasking.			
Clarify instructions and standards.			
Schedule realistic periods with times for transitions.			
Delegate tasks appropriate to my role/responsibility.			
Work when most alert and take brief breaks.			
Practice saying no nicely but firmly.			
Allow time to check accuracy/completeness.			

Michael Dell's Activities Success Story

"The whole thing was one big experiment. I learned many valuable lessons along the way. Take delegation, for example. Since I had been a college student, I was used to a schedule that allowed me to sleep late. When I started the Dell computer business, it was tough to get up early every morning. But I was the guy with the key, so if I overslept, there would be twenty or thirty employees hanging around outside the door by the time I arrived, waiting for me to let them in. When I started the company, I rarely got the door open before nine-thirty. Then it was nine o'clock. Finally, we got started at eight in the morning ... and then I gave someone else the key. Another time, I was in my office, busily trying to solve a complicated system problem when an employee walked in, complaining that he had just lost a quarter in the Coke machine. 'Why are you telling me about it?' I asked. 'Because you've got the key to the Coke machine.' At that moment, I learned the value of giving someone else the key to the Coke machine." (Dell, 1999)

Like Michael Dell, many entrepreneurs find it difficult to change from the habits that accounted for their past success to new behaviors, such as delegation. However, when times changed, this innovator had to delegate to maintain his creativity and productivity—as well as his staff's morale.

THE SPACES DEMON

The Spaces Demon lurks where we live, work, or play. Being distracted by sights and sounds, or wallowing in messy, unpleasant settings leads to feeling overwhelmed, to inaccurate work, and to a slower pace.

7

Actions Against the Spaces Demon

Dan, a home-based health food distributor, works in his bedroom, among all his boxes, books, files, and disordered heaps of papers. Various supplies are scattered in different parts of the house. He can't seem to get organized. Although he begins each week with good intentions, inevitably things begin to unravel by Wednesday. Increasingly frazzled, he wastes time locating misplaced checks, letters, and statements. The last straw? Discovering a package for a two-week-old order buried under the cleaning in the trunk of his car. His significant other suggests (for the hundredth time) that he will save time and be less distracted if he hires a part-time student to help organize his workspace. Now, for two hours a day every Wednesday and Thursday, the student organizes papers, enters data, and files receipts. Dan focuses on marketing and, as a result, is seeing his profits rise. The bonus? He feels less hassled and more likely to take the time he needs to rest or exercise.

According to estimates, more than nine and one-half million Americans work from home, and fifty percent of all small businesses are home based (Baker, 2006). Projections indicate that these figures will grow steadily. Benefits include no office rent, no commuting costs, no rigid schedules, and no high clothing costs. To engage with contacts and colleagues, you turn to no-cost social networking that's easy to use.

However, running a home business presents inherent difficulties. At home, you lack the time structure, space limits, and defined work processes imposed in a traditional business setting. At home, it's easy to get distracted and fritter away the hours in any number of nonbusiness-related activities. Dan represents the average person who works at home, according to the National Association of Professional Organizers. This organization reports that paper clutter is the number-one problem for most businesses; on average, a person loses one hour of productivity each day due to that clutter. Not a small matter.

This chapter provides charts, checklists, and tips for a Plan of Attack against distractions when working and conducting meetings. It addresses clutter, positive work conditions, and assertiveness when working in less-than-ideal spaces.

Struggles with the Spaces Demon

Whether in an open space such as a cubicle, an enclosed corporate or home office, or a shared workstation, the conditions in your workspace can help or hinder your productivity. Your goal? To create a space that makes your desk, cubicle, or office comfortable and distraction-free.

At the very least, you want to become aware of how your space affects your concentration. For example, messy desks and closets, disorganized files, intrusive noise, or offensive smells contribute to an unpleasant atmosphere. But they're more than unpleasant; they function as distracters. Often, in subtle but pervasive ways, they decrease the rate and efficiency of your performance—and increase your stress in the process.

Yes, the Spaces Demon attacks with disruptive sights, sounds, and conditions where you work or play. Plus it sets the stage for other demons like the Stress or Fatigue Demon to interfere with your efforts.

Self-Check: Your Spaces and Places

Directions: Read each statement and place a check next to all that apply to you. Visualize events that occurred over the past weeks. Next to each statement, note the degree to which you were distracted or interrupted; mark an R for rarely, an S for sometimes, or an O for often.

____ 1. I lack organized supplies in my workspace.

____ 2. I don't take time to file and organize papers/correspondence.

____ 3. I become distracted because of extraneous noises and/or others' voices.

____ 4. I can't concentrate during meetings due to distracting sights, lights, or sounds.

___ 5. I lack routines when I'm in unfamiliar surroundings, so I lose things or waste time.

___ 6. I lose time and/or money because of various distractions in my workspace.

Most people can identify at least one aspect of their work/life space that needs improving. You can have more control over the conditions you identified than you might assume.

Consequences of the Spaces Demon

In general, a direct relationship exists between productivity and clutter. As an article titled "Reducing Office Clutter" says, "Productivity and profitability decline when clutter and chaos reign" (Heydlauff, 2009). And 25 percent of those employed outside the home do some or all of their work at home (Bureau of Labor Statistics, 2010).

In a home environment, an excessive amount of clutter can accumulate. For example, the US Department of Labor reports that one-quarter of people with two-car garages have so much stuff in them that they can't park a car. This situation can be especially tricky when the garage is filled with inventory and supplies for a home business. For those living in harsh winter climates, garage clutter can not only be distracting, but inconvenience and stress build when it's freezing, snowing, sleeting, or hailing.

Assess: Is Clutter Corrupting Your Productivity?

"Things tend to pile up until one day, I just avoid a project completely," laments Leona, a mechanical engineer. Would you say that about your workspace? How effectively is it working for you? To find out, take a minute to look around your office or workspace. Sketch or photograph your current space reality and then evaluate how it helps or hinders your productivity. Take close-up photos of one or two spaces that need to be cleared of clutter, or use the space below to sketch ways to improve the effectiveness of your workspace.

When it comes to messy spaces, many people just freeze. The thought of attacking piles of papers overwhelms them so much, they shut down. Perhaps it's due to an inability to stop a rigid, all-or-none tendency or to break tasks down into more doable parts. You might have heard statements like, "I can't just clean the entire closet; I've got to do the whole room," or "I don't know where to start."

If you have similar difficulties, start with small goals. For example, say, "I'll only spend one hour clearing the closet floor." Put aside another hour one day a week to clear another area. If you have difficulty, call on a friend or professional organizer to get you going. (You'll find organizers in your area listed at www.napo.net.)

Personal Consequences of the Spaces Demon

You've probably seen how clutter within your work/life spaces can clog your mental processes. The more stuff is strewn around, the more difficulty you'll have concentrating and organizing your thoughts and materials. The more the clutter, the greater the stress, the smaller the productivity—count on it!

Describe the negative health, performance, or social consequences you experience as a result of the Spaces Demon. Rate the degree of negative consequence on a scale from one to ten, with ten being the highest degree.

Identifying Negative Consequences of the Spaces Demon

Places in Which the Spaces Demon Interferes with Productivity	Negative Health Consequences	Negative Productivity Consequences	Negative Social Consequences
1.			
2.			
3.			

Become mindful of how spaces tend to trigger distractions by addressing questions such as:

- What are my most common triggers for distraction within the spaces where I work or play?

_____

_____

- When, where, and how do spaces, or conditions within them, have a negative effect on my attention?

_____

_____

- What am I doing currently to manage spaces? In what ways are my solutions working? How do I feel about these situations?

_____

_____

Use your notes to set goals that will reduce the effects of the Spaces Demon and increase your productivity.

Set Realistic Goals to Control the Spaces Demon

Your goal may start with a statement like "Stop procrastinating! I need to take measures to protect client confidentiality and avoid security breaches." Then you'd become more specific and positive by saying, "I'll put the cell phone alarm on fifteen minutes before I plan to leave. The alarm will signal me to file papers around me and lock my clients' folders in the file cabinet." Or say, "I feel like I'm drowning in a sea of paper. I'll organize one section of my desk during the next fifteen minutes."

Visualize or review your weekly schedule to identify time for reducing your vulnerability to the Spaces Demon. What will you say or do to ensure you have positive, non-distracting work/life spaces?

- At work _____

- At home _____

- Other setting _____

Major Strategy: Develop Routines to Straighten the Mess

If you feel buried under a daily avalanche of paper and information, you're not alone. The average businessperson receives more than 10 pieces of information each day and wastes about 150 hours each year looking for stuff. (For a humorous description, watch comedian George Carlin's skits about "stuff" on YouTube.)

Not only do many people feel overwhelmed by the materials that arrive each day, they can't part with old books, magazines, receipts, or school papers. They don't have a junk drawer; they have a junk house. In extreme cases of clutter invasion, excess becomes a health and safety hazard.

You'll definitely benefit from setting "straighten the mess" goals and developing strategies and routines that work for you. A reminder about goals: The smaller the goal, the more likely you are to begin. These simple steps give you a specific goal and an immediate way of measuring progress.

1. Take a few photographs of places that are messy.

2. Divide the photo into quadrants and begin working on one section at a time.

3. Use a divide-and-conquer strategy. (Decluttering something like an entire closet or desk might seem so overwhelming that you don't start.).

4. Check one or more of these strategies you're willing to do within the next week or two to curb distractions triggered by unsightly workspaces:

___ Delineate or color-code specific work areas or storage zones.

___ Break work activities into mini tasks and schedule a "clean up mess" period for twenty to forty minutes.

___ Allot five minutes before and after each activity to straighten or file materials.

___ Create a routine for storing or filing papers and products.

___ Use three-ring binders for special projects. Label and store them in an accessible place.

___ Allot ten to fifteen minutes each week to sort, organize, and/or file papers, reports, magazines, and hard copies of your computer work.

___ Finish doing one task or activity at a time. Talk yourself through the "routine."

___ Create a checklist, and post it in a visible place.

___ Get a mess buddy who will motivate you, or hire a helper to come once a week or month to help straighten that mess.

___ Post announcements and important reminders on a bulletin board so they won't get lost.

When you feel overwhelmed, you may stall, lacking initiative. Good intention abounds, but no action results. How do you get yourself started? Try these ideas.

• Limit the scope of the project by divvying up the times you work on the task.

• Assign a block of time for filing, another block for doing your correspondence. Be kind in your self-judgment and say, "These kinds of tasks are not my thing, but they need to be done. Even a few minutes each day helps."

As your business grows, consider delegating the mundane tasks. Hire an extra set of hands to do administrative work. For some, organizing is a natural strength; for others it must be learned and practiced. When you want to improve your own organizing skills, depend on your natural strengths and learning style. For example, if you're a visual person, use photos, graphic icons, or color-coding when making files and labeling storage bins.

Some people have persistent, long-standing clutter problems that undermine their work/life. They can benefit from teleclasses on the topic, from help by those associated with organizations like the National Study Group on Chronic Disorganization (www.nsged.net), or from books on the topic, such as *Conquering Chronic Disorganization* (Kolberg, 1999).

Social support can provide the boost you need to tackle a *clutter catastrophe*. Call in a friend or a professional to help you straighten closets or basements. Use the rule, "If you haven't used it in two years, store it, sell it, donate it, or throw it away." For those who love to save everything, the rule is "If you haven't seen it in ten years …"

Write down your ideas about ways you can get help (beg, barter, buy) to straighten out your mess:

• _____

• _____

• _____

In addition, organizing tools can help. For example, find inexpensive closet organizers to store your equipment and accessories. Too often, cords, adapters, and chargers clutter your drawers and closets, and you waste valuable time hunting for the piece you need. Using a hanging shoe or sweater holder can be invaluable.

Whether at the office or at home, plan regular times during the year to de-clutter, selecting at least one activity each quarter or during vacation or holiday time. Here's a sample chart you can use to get started.

Decluttering at Regular Intervals

	1st Quarter	2nd Quarter	3rd Quarter	4th Quarter
Clean supply closets.				
Service/clean car.				
Clear out file cabinets.				
Reorganize bookshelves.				
Clean out and wash cabinets/ drawers.				
Other				
Other				
Other				
Other				

Issue: Messy Desk, Messy Mind?

You walk into a manager's office and notice piles of paper on the desk and floor; files are strewn around the cabinet. You think, *What a mess! This manager must be a ditz.* However, when you ask for a particular report, Mr. Mess goes to a pile, shuffles through a few layers, and hands you exactly what you want. You're astounded.

In this case, a messy desk doesn't indicate a messy mind. This manager has a visual image of where each item is located. He puts his hand out and grabs what he wants. In fact, the clutter might give him comfort rather than distract him. He's someone who enjoys seeing and knowing where everything is. In such cases, stacks of documents, files, and open books might trigger his memory, attention, and action. The Spaces Demon doesn't act as a barrier to this manager's performance.

For others, however, the mess reflects a vulnerability in their ability to organize. They fight a constant battle to control the clutter within their work/life spaces. For some, a messy desk reflects some messiness in their visual or organizational thinking or executive functioning. They face any number of vulnerabilities, including:

- Prioritizing: identifying the most important or time-sensitive tasks that require completion

- Sequencing: arranging items or ideas in a logical order

- Managing time: being aware of schedules and keeping on track

- Visualizing the big picture: being able to discern the "forest" from the "trees"

- Visual memory and organization: being able to organize and find objects in space

When things get out of order, most people feel overwhelmed and stressed. Commonly, they avoid the task, and things get worse. The clutter functions as a distraction and impedes their productivity—and sanity.

For still others, distraction triggers a cycle of disorganization and forgetfulness. Here's how the cycle operates.

> *You're working at your desk and holding a tax refund check. You're distracted when the phone rings in another room. You drop the check on the desk and run to answer the call. Next to the telephone is a stack of bills. You get distracted when you notice a due date and realize that one bill is almost overdue. You grab the bills and dump the pile on top of the check. Later, you remember you haven't dealt with the check and feel irritated when you can't find it. Frustration mounts because incidents like this occur day after day. In this cycle, distraction breeds disorganization, and then disorganization triggers more distraction, negatively affecting both your memory and motivation.*

Issue and Strategies: Meetings

Millions of meetings are conducted every day across the nation—about eleven million each day. Busy professionals attend over sixty meetings a month (https://e-meetings. verizonbusiness.com/global/en/meetingsinamerica/uswhitepaper.php).

Meetings, at work or outside of the work setting, can be riddled with distractions—people arrive late, don't have agendas, and wander off-topic, making it difficult to think and get anything done. In a Microsoft survey (Microsoft, 2005), employees cited wasteful meetings as the biggest productivity killer in their workday.

Have you noticed that meetings conducted in restaurants can be especially difficult? Participants deal with an onslaught of distractions, including a crowded physical layout, loud music, interruptions by servers, even extremes in temperature. What can you do? Stop distractions by establishing routines. For example, ring a bell or tone to begin the meeting, plan the agenda with time slots for each item, appoint someone to take notes, and allow five minutes for members to organize their notes or plan future meetings before ending it. In general, pledge to schedule fewer meetings, and reduce the time allotted for one meeting by at least ten minutes. Always build in time for breaks and transitions.

In many eating establishments, the music or television blares, distracting customers and inhibiting an easy flow of conversation. If the noise level hampers your effectiveness or enjoyment when meeting and dining, assertively request what you need. Say, "We're having an important meeting. It would be helpful if you would lower the volume of the music or turn it off." Sometimes managers react more positively to such requests when you add, "I think someone in the group is hard of hearing." When you insist on a quiet atmosphere, you're helping those who have hearing problems but feel embarrassed to speak up.

When you are in charge of planning a business meeting, use a checklist to set up and make your meetings effective. A great resource is, *Boring Meetings Suck: Get More Out of Your Meetings, or Get Out of More Meetings* (Petz, 2011).

Checklist: Ten Conditions for Positive Meetings

_____ 1. Adequate lighting to facilitate easy reading

_____ 2. Ample space on table tops to allow for spreading out papers

_____ 3. Ample space between tables to ensure privacy

_____ 4. Comfortable chairs to avoid aches and fatigue

_____ 5. Moderate temperature and a thermostat that can be adjusted

_____ 6. No music or low-volume music

_____ 7. Acoustic ceiling that softens noise, allowing for speaking at a natural volume

_____ 8. Options for those with special dietary needs

_____ 9. Alert and gracious receptionist, manager, and wait staff

_____ 10. Availability of private space for confidential discussions

Your goal is to optimize the conditions within the spaces you meet. The fewer distractions, the more you and your group can accomplish.

When you participate in a second meeting, take a few minutes to relax, transition to the new space, and get on track. Although you've already taken your seat, often your mind still buzzes about details of the last meeting, especially if it was filled with conflict. Resting for even a few minutes between meetings allows you to regain your focus so you can deal with the issues at hand.

Increasingly, businesses conduct online meetings. Unfortunately, group members online might be simultaneously answering e-mails, doing crossword puzzles, or playing games. When possible, schedule video conferences to reduce such inattention. Discuss ways to streamline the online meetings with your group. For example, plan shorter agendas, propose specific time slots, appoint a timekeeper, and pledge to give undivided attention to the issues being discussed. Shortening the time by even a few minutes gives participants time to write notes, make telephone calls, or engage in pressing follow-up activities.

Issues and Strategies: Office Spaces

Walk through the corridor of cubicles in any office and you'll be impressed by the striking uniqueness of each space. The decorations you see reflect each employee's specific needs and learning styles.

Two aspects of such workspaces stand out—first, the photos and memorabilia that add personality and comfort, and second, the supplies to complete tasks and enhance productivity. Do you give conscious thought to arranging the items in your space so they help you concentrate? For example, photos can provide a brief pleasant break, but if they trigger daydreaming when you're working, move them out of your range of vision.

In addition, ask, "Is there a relationship between the space in which I'm working and the type of activity that needs completing?" Perhaps you need to shift your workplace when delving into a particular type of activity. For example, Jerome, a graduate student, finds it most productive to work in the library when doing research, in a coffee shop when writing, and at home when analyzing data. He shifts according to his need for resources, his alertness, and the type of activity that needs to be done. Similarly, one lawyer in a busy, noisy firm gets away from office-centered distractions by going to the public library. He spends hours holed up in a quiet room, completing his work without interruptions. Another professional frequents a coffee shop that doesn't offer Wifi so he's not tempted to go on the Internet when he's developing a budget.

Consider the location of noisy machines like copiers and the amount of foot traffic they create. Are they close to your workspace? Sometimes, reorganizing your space, moving supplies and equipment, or using a screen helps decrease distractions.

Spend a few minutes identifying places you deem most conducive to completing particular tasks. Write down your ideas here.

Location 1: _____ Best space to do: _____

Location 2: _____ Best space to do: _____

Issue and Strategies: Stop the Sensory Bombardment

Many people can't stand the assault on their senses when walking down a busy city street. Yet, their work or home environments can be as chaotic as the corner of Forty-Second Street and Broadway in New York City. They are bombarded by sights, lights, smells, people, and, of course, noise: blaring horns, sirens, ringing, and talking. Noise is one of the most distracting realities in our work/life settings.

In general, noise negatively affects your heart rate, blood pressure, vasoconstriction, and stress hormone levels, while increasing your risk of heart attack (Prochnik, 2010). There's even an annual Noise Awareness Day in May to draw attention to this problem. Ever since open designs in offices became popular, noise has been a major source of distraction and frustration.

For years, however, the severity of this problem went unrecognized by leaders. For example, in one study, although 70 percent of office workers polled said that productivity would increase if office noise would decrease, 81 percent of executives reported they were not concerned with office noises. Yet according to experts, low-level noise causes stress and factors into decreased productivity. Psychologists report the harmful effects of noise on general cognition and health (Novotney, 2011). Novotney's work, for example, explores how noise pollution can lead to higher blood pressure and fatal heart attacks. In addition, his article "Get Your Clients Moving: Ten tips to incorporate exercise into your treatment arsenal" reports that chronic noise impairs a child's development of cognitive and language skills when houses or schools are near airport flight paths, railways, or highways.

If noise is a primary or even subtle source of distraction for you, make a list of the sounds that interfere with your productivity and identify ways you might make a change. For example, using earplugs or headphones can result in better focus, especially when you're completing an arduous task. You can also schedule a quiet or meditative time to improve your ability to be productive. Some office settings use sound-masking devices to reduce distraction and ensure confidentiality (Carsia, 2002).

Once you're aware of the noises or visual distractions that impede you, make a goal to reduce them. Review this list and check the tips you're willing to try within your work setting during the next week.

In your cubicle or office

_____ Use sound-masking devices to mask noise.

_____ Add a small fan to provide white noise.

_____ Wear earplugs or noise-canceling earphones (if allowed by work rules).

_____ Listen to soft music through earphones (if allowed by work rules).

_____ Ask managers to make changes or set policies to improve a noisy environment.

It's important to increase silence as well as decrease noise. In fact, the importance of quiet time is being recognized. Several commuter railroads now designate one or more cars as quiet cars. For example, in Chicago, quiet cars in which passengers are required to mute electronics and silence cell phones are available on all lines (Groeninger and Black, 2011).

Issue and Strategies: Assertiveness in Shared Spaces

Conflict often occurs when people with different personal styles share space, whether in the cubicle or the kitchen. You have a right to a visually pleasing and pleasant space—at least part of the time. With a new office mate, roommate, or significant other, you may confront the challenge of different needs and styles. Within shared workspaces, little things mean a lot. Here's a case in point.

> *As college sophomores living on their own for the first time, George and Jack are a younger version of the 1960s' play "The Odd Couple." Similar to Oscar, George is oblivious to messes, while Jack, like Felix, is a neat freak. Whenever George has a late-night snack, he leaves the dishes and spills on the counter for Jack to face in the morning, a time when he likes to study. But Jack can't concentrate because of the mess. Jack doesn't want to make a big deal out of it, but given his need for orderliness, he finds himself irritated and stressed, snapping at George without explaining why. He goes to class mumbling about how he can't stand the way George acts. Jack's stress rises. George can't figure out the reason for Jack's grumpiness. Finally, Jack gets up his nerve and describes his need for orderliness. As a result, George is willing to take a stab at remedying the situation. Here's the contract the two devised:*
>
> *Goal: To have a clean kitchen counter in the morning*
>
> *Positive Outcomes: Greater enjoyment of shared space, less irritation and stress, more positive atmosphere, and better interpersonal interactions.*
>
> *New routine: George posts a sign on his bedroom door as a reminder to clear the counter if he has a snack in the evening. Jack thanks George for his consideration and stops snapping at him in the morning.*

In this situation, Jack uses his assertive skills to talk about the situation, reducing tension and making sure his studying gets done. Whether dealing with the *Others* Demon, the Spaces Demon or the Stress Demon, assertive skills can help you prevent distractions from impairing you productivity.

Use Demon-Defying Strategies

You're drowning in papers; you're constantly interrupted by noise, others, and social media. You feel frustrated. Consider adopting the following strategies to reduce distraction and increase your productivity and profitability:

___ *Use visualization.* Imagine how your office might be rearranged to decrease the number of visual distractions and make it easier to put your hands on records and supplies. For help, talk to others about their space arrangements, contact an organizer, or go online to research the topic of organization.

___ *Use reason.* It's only common sense; you can't make a profit if you don't spend quality think time to clear the clutter, organize a budget, market your services/products, deal with customers, and plan strategically. Do one thing at a time, take a break, and move on—while tracking your progress and profits, the positive results of your business.

___ *Use constructive self-talk.* Give yourself a pep talk. Say, "I can organize in a better way. I've done it before. I just need to rearrange things and spend time every month keeping the organization going."

___ *Use positive assertiveness.* Post signs, send out e-mails, and provide personal requests to family and friends about good times to contact you rather than interrupting you.

___ *Institute productive routines.* Allow five to ten minutes before and after the day's activities to clear your desk, file papers, and list tasks to accomplish. Place your task list in a visible place or put it into your PDA.

___ *Use the Stop, Look, and Listen technique.* Pose this question, "Given the work I need to complete, should I move my workspace to ensure a distraction-free setting?" Stop for a few minutes to review your productivity. Look with your mind's eye at where you currently work and visualize a more productive setting for accomplishing particular activities. Listen to your internal dialogue about what you should or could do. Heed your own advice. For example, say, "I let these mounds of papers grow over several years; I don't have to clear it all in one day."

___ *Access social support.* Networking is a critical component of your business program, especially if you have a home-based business. Consider lunch or coffee dates with other business owners, a local business or networking group, or an online business network like LinkedIn.

Moving from Intention to Action

Taking action against the Spaces Demon requires making conscious choices to set goals, keep track of activities, and recognize and reward your progress. Is there a space in your work/life that fosters disruption? What commitment to change might you consider? Do you need to use positive assertiveness skills to attain your goal?

Following these steps can enhance your progress on the issues you identified.

1. *Assess.* Visualize work/life areas in which your productivity lags due to distraction, disorganization, excessive stimuli, or an unpleasant atmosphere. Ask, "How does the Spaces Demon interfere with my work/life productivity?" Write down your answer here.

_____

_____

_____

2. *Analyze consequences.* List the costs and consequences of distractions within the spaces you work or play. Determine what's wasted due to conditions that divert your attention. Ask, "As I work in various spaces, how do I waste time, effort, or money?" Be specific; list the benefits you'll realize if you reduce distractions within and around your workspace.

_____

_____

_____

3. *Set realistic goals.* Reflect on ways to rearrange distracting conditions in your work/life spaces to improve your performance and decrease your stress. Ask, "What one or two behaviors will help me reduce distracting conditions and increase my productivity?" You might state goals in general terms (e.g., increase productivity and profitability; keep records confidential and secure; reduce stress, overwhelm, and errors) and then become more specific (e.g., commit to filing all tax information containing social security numbers in a locked cabinet every day). Write down your specific goals or new behaviors here.

_____

_____

_____

4. *Take action.* Identify strategies to decrease distractions at work and at home. Ask, "When, where, and how will I move from intention to action?" and "What specific strategies or tips will I use?" Write down your strategies here.

_____

_____

_____

5. *Monitor and maintain progress.* While you're clearing the clutter or organizing your space, stay on track by congratulating yourself with small rewards. To some people, this idea sounds ridiculous. They say, "Why do I need rewards? Isn't this what I'm supposed to be doing anyway?" Although it appears simplistic, the more you reward and recognize your efforts, the more likely you'll continue doing chores that don't appeal to you. Write down your thoughts here.

_____

_____

_____

Using a checklist helps you monitor progress, stay on target, and identify occasions to praise your efforts and achievements. The following chart can help with your Plan of Attack against the Spaces Demon.

Actions Against the Spaces Demon

	Work	Home	Other
Set a time to clear the clutter.			
Create a non-distracting space.			
Post signs: Do Not Disturb.			
Use a comfortable, supportive chair.			
Regulate the temperature and possibly use a fan.			
Organize materials/supplies.			
Provide ample non-glare light.			
Other			

When you keep track of your progress, you increase the chances you'll improve or adjust when necessary. Be creative. Devise ways that are both appealing and enjoyable for you.

Louise's Spaces Success Story

Inspired by a teleseminar, I decided to try a new approach to deal with my "clutter catastrophe." The next day, I started to organize the barn. I've wanted to do it for more than three years. Previously, whenever I had started to clean, I couldn't work for long because the barn is dark, depressing, smelly, infested, and, worst of all, filled with too many memories. It had never occurred to me to decorate the barn while I was straightening it out. After all, why should I decorate it when I'm not using it?

Nevertheless, I followed the advice from the teleseminar to create a pleasant atmosphere and follow a systematic process. Because I enjoy decorating, it helped me get this job done. I put on music, dragged out several lamps and extension cords, and placed them around so I could see. After that, I approached the task with determination and decorated the first floor in less than a half hour. As a result, cleaning out the attic area took fewer than three days. Usually, seeing my mother's metal birdhouse makes me cry, but I stuck a big yellow flower in it and hung it up from the rafter. Now it makes me smile.

Today, my barn looks like a country store with all sorts of interesting things hanging from the ceiling. I even made a scarecrow outside.

By following a step-by-step process and making the task more enjoyable, Louise got motivated to tackle her long-delayed clear-the-clutter project. She discovered that, given the right circumstances, an odious job can be completed in less time than she'd ever imagined.

THE STRESS DEMON

The Stress Demon can be activated by internal or external triggers, robbing us of the psychic energy needed to pay attention. Without conscious attention to stress management, we make too many mistakes.

8

Actions Against the Stress Demon

Kristen completes her residency in orthopedic surgery and plans to move out of town to a new job. Although she's competent, she's hassled because of upcoming specialty board examinations, wedding plans, and a new job. Already tired from the rigors of the past nine years of training, she feels overwhelmed by all she needs to do in a few short weeks. She stays up even later than normal, skips meals, and snaps at coworkers, friends, and family. As her stress level increases, Kristen's attention to detail, memory, and organization decrease. For example, she forgets to call the dressmaker and doesn't pick up a dress she needs for her wedding shower. More important, she loses the check required by the medical licensing board in the state where she is moving. Also, she's unaware of how her stress is undermining her enjoyment of this wonderful time. Her fiancé keeps saying, "What's going on? You're a wreck! You need to relax."

During this time of excitement, Kristen is experiencing slippages in her performance due to distraction attacks. One might not relate stress to happy events, but whenever uncertainty is afoot, it's easy to feel uncomfortable and stressed.

Stress is the body's natural reaction to real or perceived danger. When endangered, your body's survival mechanism goes into a *fight-or-flight* response. A surge of adrenaline and other stress hormones pump through your body so you can respond to that perceived danger.

Too frequently, however, this response gets misused or overused. Everything in your life feels like an emergency, even events that aren't life-threatening—the false alarms. Yet a continuous cycle of stress can become entrenched, exhausting your mental and emotional resources. At that point, sliding into ineffective performance and burnout comes easily.

Studies estimate that 75 percent of the population experiences at least some stress every two weeks, with half feeling moderate or high levels of stress during the two-week period. Although many people accept stress as part of contemporary life, a high amount of stress endangers the health and welfare of the overall population.

This chapter provides charts, checklists, and tips to help you make a Plan of Attack against distractions due to situational work/life stress. It addresses social issues, including distorted thinking, perfectionism, and caregiving.

The Stress Mess

As exemplified by Kristen's story, stress clearly affects attention, memory, organization, and effectiveness. In addition, when you feel stressed, you lack the energy to tackle such chores as clearing the clutter, organizing supplies, shopping for groceries, or doing laundry. Disorganization dominates. The increased mess leads to more stress and less energy for attention and memory. A daily or weekly dose of stress management can provide the impetus to minimize disorganization and forgetfulness.

No one is immune from the affects of negative stress. Even those with high intellectual potential and well-developed coping skills can be brought to their emotional knees by the stress associated with their own (or another's) life changes, including illness, death, or financial setback.

Life interrupts life. Of the top-ten causes of stress, check all that you have endured in the last twelve months.

___ Onset of an illness or management of a chronic disease

___ Serious illness or accident of a loved one

___ Departure or death of a partner, family member, or dear friend

___ Change or loss of job

___ Change of residence or place of business

___ Home or business reconstruction projects

___ Financial setback or economic downturn

___ Change in marital status: marriage, separation, divorce, death, or affair

___ Introduction of a child into one's life through birth, foster care, or adoption

___ Feelings of social, career, or personal failure

When excess stress mercilessly inflicts its damage, your attention defenses plummet; you become especially vulnerable to distraction. Preoccupied by worry, you may spin your wheels and ignore critical but seemingly less-pressing activities like exercise and safety.

Although you expect to feel stressed during crisis situations, you might overlook the stress that comes with anticipated changes, transitions, or even joyous events. Like Kristen, you might not be aware of the taxing effects of dealing with multiple life changes. You neglect your physical and emotional needs; you fail to focus on details; you have trouble paying attention. Consequently, you get in an accident, make a mistake, or lose such important items as a check or legal document.

Remember, the greater the stress, the lower your capacity to focus, remember, organize, and motivate.

Self-Check: The Stress Mess

Directions: Read each statement and check all statements that apply to you. Visualize events that occurred over the past weeks and then indicate the degree to which you were distracted by stress using a letter designation: *R* for rarely, *S* for sometimes, and *O* for often.

___ 1. I feel stressed before I begin certain tasks.

___ 2. I experience intrusive thoughts when I try to pay attention for any length of time.

___ 3. I have to stop an activity because of symptoms of stress, such as a headache or nervous stomach.

___ 4. I'm jumpy and can't seem to concentrate long enough to read instructions or do chores.

___ 5. Others say I'm moody and irritable, that I appear stressed.

___ 6. When I feel stressed, I suffer more disorganization and forgetfulness than normal.

If you checked more than one or two items, you could be experiencing a degree of stress that interferes with your performance. Talk about your results with a friend or counselor who can help you decide how to reduce your stress in particular situations.

General Consequences of Stress

People around the globe suffer at the hands of the Stress Demon. For example, in Australia, the United States, the United Kingdom, and Germany, the costs of job-related stress range from $200 to $300 billion annually (http://stress.healthytreatment.com/statistics-regarding-stress-worldwide-epidemic/). The losses are reflected in absenteeism, low productivity, employee turnover, accidents, various fees—medical, legal, insurance—and so on.

Recently, throughout the United States, stress in the workplace has reached an all-time high (American Psychological Association, 2010). Employers are advised to pay attention to the disastrous effects of job-related stress if they want healthier employees and bigger profits (Centazzo, 2008). Studies show stress tends to account for between 60 to 90 percent of all medical office visits in the United States. According to the National Institute for Occupational Safety and Health, stress also correlates to risks of cardiovascular disease, back and upper-extremity disorders, depression and burnout, workplace injury, and ulcers

(http://www.holisticservices.com, 2004; http://www.free-health-advice.com/articles/stress/stress-statistics.html) (4/23/2009).

Although you might consider stress a natural part of work/life, it's especially acute for individuals who worry about finances, health, or family problems. Indeed, for those caught in distressing economic times, stress levels can skyrocket. A survey featured in the January 2011 issue of *Monitor on Psychology* reports, "Most Americans are suffering from moderate to high stress, with 44 percent reporting that their stress levels have increased over the past five years." In addition, the report states that many Americans aren't coping well with their stress. They're unhappy about their level of exercise, overeating, or eating unhealthy foods (Anderson, 2011).

Assess: Keep a Stress Diary

Like others, you may have long-standing patterns for dealing with unpleasant events that can cause stress. For example, procrastination is a common way for people to postpone feeling stressed. The cycle begins by putting off a task that's aversive, boring, or difficult. When a deadline hovers, though, you become more acutely aware of the negative consequences if the task isn't completed. The perceived threat of those consequences triggers an adrenaline rush that helps you focus your attention and take action. Do you recall being a student, when "pulling an all-nighter" produced a quick, usually positive result, like passing a test? But when completing important work/life tasks, recognize procrastination that leads to all-nighters as unproductive. Over the long haul, working under time pressures can be debilitating. In effect, you become your worst enemy. But knowing the enemy is half the battle.

Ask, "What are my patterns and the stress consequences of those patterns over time?" To answer these questions, keep a stress-awareness diary for a week or two. Follow these steps.

1. Note the day and time a stressful event occurs.

2. Visualize the stress episode and identify the physical or emotional stress symptoms you experienced. Note any inability to concentrate or such symptoms as irritability, restlessness, headaches, tightness in your neck, and so on.

3. Note the conditions that exist before and after the stressful reactions you identified. Ask, "What happened just before I felt stressed? Did I begin to worry that my work isn't good enough? Is perfectionism impeding my performance? Is it triggering unnecessary stress?"

4. Review when and for how long you experience stress during a day or week. Then consider how the stress affects your ability to pay attention to and complete critical tasks. Always ask, "What are the consequences of my stress pattern?"

Journal: Stress Triggers

Day/Time	Place	Stress Episode	Symptom(s)	What Triggered the Stress?	What Happened after the Stress?

Take time to become mindful of how stress triggers distraction for you by addressing such questions as:

*   What are my most common triggers for stress?

_____

_____

- When, where, and how does stress negatively affect my attention?

  _____

  _____

- What am I doing to improve the stressful situation? In what ways are my solutions working? How do I feel about these situations?

  _____

  _____

- Am I seeking relief from stress by over- or under-eating or excessively smoking, drinking, or indulging in other negative habits?

  _____

  _____

- How serious are these distractions at work or home on a scale from one to ten, with ten indicating the most serious?

Work: 1	2	3	4	5	6	7	8	9	10
Home: 1	2	3	4	5	6	7	8	9	10
Other: 1	2	3	4	5	6	7	8	9	10

Note the times you felt relatively stress-free, then include more of these times in your routine.

When you ask and answer questions, you're likely to identify specific consequences that influence your behavior. In turn, this information helps you think of ways to improve your performance.

Research provides data to show how people can and do manage stress. It's comforting to know that implementing strategies can make your life easier during stressful times. When you use the stress management strategies from this chapter, you decrease the chances that your performance will decline or you'll slide into a chronic stress condition. Bottom line: to avoid stress, minimize distractions, even when you're involved in dramatic or unsettling events.

Analyze Personal Consequences of Stress

Sometimes stress builds up so slowly you're not aware of the toll it takes on your work or personal life. In the chart below, note the degree of negative consequences you experience in various settings due to stress. Describe a stressful situation and then note the negative health, performance, or social consequence you experience afterward. Rate the severity of negative consequence(s) for each category using a scale from one to ten, with ten being the highest. Write the number in each box.

Identifying Negative Consequences of Stress

Stressful Situations	Negative Health Consequences	Negative Productivity Consequences	Negative Social Consequences

On her ninetieth birthday, Aunt Fritzi described her philosophy this way: "Life is a do-it-yourself project. During life's ups and downs, you need to take responsibility to work things out." In your own do-it-yourself project, ask, "Is stress interfering with my productivity and satisfaction? Is it distracting me from my life goals?" If you answer yes, determine the degree to which it undermines your performance. If you have constant trouble doing everyday tasks, are worrying about getting through the day and thinking things will always go badly, you could be suffering from anxiety (National Institute of Mental Health, 2007). Check with your doctor or mental health professional. Be honest with yourself. Make a list of your symptoms before your appointment—if the exercise doesn't create too much stress!

Set Realistic Goals to Defuse the Stress Demon

It's wise to note the times during the week when you feel relatively stress-free. By asking and answering questions, you're likely to identify conditions that influence your behavior. In turn, this information promotes thinking of ways to improve your performance.

What small, simple goals might you set for yourself to minimize distractions? Try the following to reduce the impact of your stress-related distractions.

- Schedule at least fifteen minutes each day for de-stressing.

- Commit to using strategies that lead to de-stressing.

- Experiment with stress management strategies that are new to you.

Visualize or review your weekly schedule to identify goals for reducing your vulnerability to the Stress Demon and giving yourself time to calm down. Write down specific details about what you can do.

- At work _____

- At home _____

- Other setting _____

Major Stress Management Strategies

Although you can't always avoid stress, you can anticipate, manage, and stop it from spiraling out of control. Yes, you *can* deal with the potential negative forces of stress in an increasingly complex, fast-paced, and distracting world.

- Be aware of and respect the Stress Demon as a worthy adversary.

- Identify what triggers your stress at work and at home.

- Routinely use proven stress-management strategies.

- Be ready to reach out to others for help when the Stress Demon attacks.

The strategies you use depend on your strengths and interests. Experiment with a variety of them to discover those that are most effective for you. Be sure to combine strategies from other chapters to combat everyday stresses and strains. For example, you might employ humor for mildly irritating situations but rely on yoga or exercise for ongoing stress management.

Consider implementing some or all of these six widely accepted stress-management strategies.

1. *Appeal to the senses.* Colors, sounds, and smells can influence your mood. Become more mindful of the ways each affects you. In terms of color, ask, "How can I infuse different hues into my work/life to help me relax or perk up?" For example, vibrant colors, such as orange, shocking pink, bright yellow and emerald green, are energizing, while soft shades of blue and green are calming. In terms of sound, ask, "What sounds might distract, calm, or energize me?"

Some people prefer the sounds of the ocean or rain, while others like hearing birds, chimes, or music. Make a conscious effort to use color and/or sound to modulate your mood. Sometimes the easiest way to relieve stress is also the cheapest and most accessible. Wear a wild and wacky shirt or tie, put out a bright tablecloth, or listen to a rousing John Philip Sousa march. You'll be surprised how effective these simple stress busters can be. In terms of fragrances, the scent of lavender can calm, while a whiff of lemon zest or evergreen can energize. It's important to identify a few simple ways to create a relaxing atmosphere. If you do an Internet search, you'll discover that the most common short-term, stress-relieving strategies involve the use of scented candles, teas, hammocks, water fountains, wind chimes, foot and neck massage devices, wind spinners, stress balls, eye masks, and aromatherapy diffusers.

2. *Access nature.* Your stress-management scheme might include being in nature—our great balancer, as Ralph Waldo Emerson said. You feel refreshed and relaxed after a brief walk in the park, by a stream, or in the mountains. You benefit from the sights, sounds, and smells of nature—whether your face is in the sun or your eyes are on the stars.

3. *Add light.* When the dark winter invades, millions of people suffer from the winter blahs. Many benefit from using artificial light to reduce the negative effects of seasonal darkness. For well over a decade, bright light treatment has been recognized as an accepted therapy for winter depression (Depression Guideline Panel, 1993). Exposure to light from a special floor lamp, box, or visor for twenty to thirty minutes is known to counteract the effects of reduced light during the winter months (www. northenlighttechnologies.com). If the winter blues get to you, contact a medical or mental health professional about your options.

4. *Use humor.* Humor and laughter are instant, powerful stress busters. When you have a good laugh, you relax tense muscles and take deep breaths. When you use humor to decrease the tension from an upsetting incident, you've identified an *antidote for angst.* When you apply lightheartedness to your own foibles, you defuse negativity, gain a fresh perspective, and reframe unpleasantness. Laughing about your mistakes makes them more manageable and less devastating.

> Use humor at home as a positive distraction. How? Keep a humor diary, and collect cartoons, jokes, and humorous quotes. Find silly toys and puzzles. Take breaks to play with toys or clay, read cartoons and jokes, take in comedy routines, etc. Be playful.

> At work, liven up those tense meetings with good-natured fun (Feigelson, 1998). Share cartoons to focus others' attention and reduce stress. The long-term popularity of cartoons such as *Doonesbury* by G. B. Trudeau, *Peanuts* by Charles Schultz, *Dilbert* by Scott Adams, and *Pot Shots* by Ashley Brilliant attests to a human need to find the humor in everyday work/life settings. Take frequent laughter breaks throughout the day and see how humor leads to greater motivation, camaraderie, and innovation.

5. *Exercise.* Want an antidote to stress and anxiety? Exercise. It's good for your

brain. Authors like John Ratey, MD (2008) have explored the connection between exercise and brain performance. In his book *SPARK: The Revolutionary New Science of Exercise and the Brain*, Dr. Ratey described how even moderate exercise supercharges mental circuits to sharpen thinking, enhance memory, and beat stress.

> Increasingly, mental health professionals are incorporating exercise into their treatment arsenal (Novotney, 2009). The prevailing wisdom is that you should engage in moderate exercise three times a week for twenty to sixty minutes each time. You can always make it more pleasant by exercising with a friend, walking a dog, or going with a colleague to a local gym.

6. *Meditate.* Doing meditation quiets the mind by focusing your attention on a repeated sound called a mantra. By meditating, you can enjoy a deeply relaxed state without distraction. It's well worth practicing every day for the peaceful benefits it produces. Some simple steps include finding a quiet spot, getting comfortable, breathing normally through your nose, turning your attention inward, moving toward stillness, and focusing on deep breathing and relaxing. Keep your attention on breathing evenly. Some people find that meditating in natural surroundings helps deepen the relaxation. Focus your attention on an object or process, such as your breathing, a word, a sound, a saying, an image, or soft music.

7. *Mindfulness.* When you fully focus on aspects of the present moment, you become less distracted and more mindful. During such times, the goal is to maintain an open and nonjudgmental attitude about your observations. When employed well, mindfulness can help you monitor and modulate your attention and help you use such strategies as visualization and positive self-talk to reduce stress.

Issue and Strategies: Distorted Thinking Opens the Door to *the Blues*

Do you inadvertently fall into the habit of using distorted thinking when your emotions get in the way of logical thought? Such thinking casts a negative (and sometimes hopeless) shadow over a situation. For example, when Carlo experienced a disappointment at work, he exacerbated his stress with all-or-none, now-or-never thinking like this: "I knew I couldn't do it. It will never be better." Falling into a *shame-and-blame* perspective, he blamed himself entirely for the situation. In turn, this reaction reduced his ability to be promoted into a problem-solving position. Most likely, Carlo could reduce his stress if he put things into a limited, positive perspective. Logical thinking can reduce his stress. For example, he might say, "Although this time it didn't work, I'll find a better way next time."

Have you noticed that generalizing or distorting the magnitude of a problem tends to increase stress? Your self-talk influences the frequency and intensity of stress.

More than that, high stress is tiring and can open the door to depression. Dealing with today's pressures, you need a handy way of sloughing off minor aggravations. Think *calm* rather than *angry* thoughts. Listen to music or read jokes or cartoons. Have on hand a few prepared statements to replace any negative statements you typically make during stressful times.

Consider this situation: while preparing your yearly tax returns, you misplace your glasses for a fourth time. You might blame yourself, saying, "Jerk! You'd lose your head if it wasn't attached to your body." Unfortunately, such statements *increase* negativity and stress. Instead, consider these positive ways of handling various situations.

- Describe the conditions and situation: "I must be nervous about finishing the taxes if I can't keep track of my glasses. I guess I'm more stressed than I thought."

- Propose a logical solution: "Perhaps I need a break. It's annoying to constantly misplace my reading glasses; I need to use an eyeglass chain."

Determine whether the stressful situation is occasional or habitual, and come up with a long-term solution. Do you need skill building, better directions, or a realignment of expectations? Should you be working with an expert to learn stress-management strategies?

Issue and Strategies: Perfectionism and Stress

It's common to lean toward perfectionism in some aspects of your life. This quality reflects your high standards, coupled with your motivation to strive for excellence. There's a danger, however, when you shift your *quest for the best* to *a need for perfection* in all endeavors.

Without a logical analysis of what you have to accomplish in relation to time, money, and energy, you could feel overwhelmed, worried about failure, and sometimes paralyzed. When these experiences occur with frequency, you might conclude, "There is no sense in trying," or "If I don't achieve the ideal, I am a failure."

Such self-talk causes stress!

You run the risk of falling into a habit of self-defeating thinking laced with pessimism. In essence, you're always beating yourself up and feeling guilty about something. You never feel *good enough*. To overcome that, balance your expectations about the way things are supposed to be with these two actions.

- Review what's reasonable, given the conditions and time constraints.

- Review the standards and best practices within your particular workplace or other situation.

When perfectionism operates, it not only triggers stress but can set in motion a chain reaction that includes failure, sadness, and more stress. At its root is the belief that you (or others) should—must—be perfect. It's an all-or-nothing pressure that defies logic. How can a person be perfect? Perfection is for the gods, and mythology tells us even the revered Greek and Roman gods were flawed.

Also, with perfectionism you harbor an irrational belief that you must do things a certain way. Your idealized vision of how things are supposed to be becomes your reality. Unfortunately, perfectionism reduces motivation and creativity, and it frequently increases procrastination.

Issue and Strategies: Stress and Caregiving

Caregiving is stressful. Caregivers report that they get less sleep, do more during the day, and get less exercise than when they were not caring for others. They tend to ignore their own needs for rest and relaxation. On an airplane, the emergency instructions are clear: take care of yourself with an oxygen mask before you help others, such as children or the elderly. On the ground, as you're managing multiple responsibilities, you might not see how much caregiving responsibilities have eroded your ability to take care of yourself. In chapter 5, Jill's story illustrated how the *Others* Demon involved caregiving. Here's an example of caregiving as it relates to the Stress Demon:

> *Anita is a high-achieving, highly stressed single parent. In addition to helping her father who's recovering from a stroke, she's working toward a promotion and worrying about company budget cuts. She skips meals, ignores her exercise routine, and gains weight. She loses both her expensive jacket and cell phone in the same week. Her sister Marsha warns her to "put on your own oxygen mask for the next few months. If you don't, how will you keep going? Besides, it's flu season. Remember that bout of walking pneumonia you had a few months ago?"*

In Anita's case, stress causes performance slippages and presents the specter of illness. To what degree is stress interfering with *your* attempts to care for yourself? How is your concern for others masking your own needs? Consider setting *take-care-of-me* goals and identify the positive consequences of achieving them. Self-care goals appear easy to attain but in reality can be highly elusive.

Regrettably, many people take better care of their pets or cars than they do of themselves. Given the hassle and stress of daily life, they berate themselves for their performance slippages—the lost key ring, the missed appointment, the cell phone that fell into the toilet. A better approach could be to accept a degree of slippage and engage in self-compassion (Weir, 2011). That means telling yourself supportive things, just as you would tell a friend who messed up. Say, "I need time for transitions without taking the cell phone everywhere I go. I'm smart, but no one is smart enough to be on the go all day long, stressing out and doing everything for everyone else every minute of the day."

Decide to slow down, rest, and de-stress for short periods during the day. Then get out of the habit of being super-critical of yourself. Remember, out there lots of unsupportive people dish out unjustified criticism every day. You don't have to be one of them—especially toward yourself.

Strategy: A "Take Better Care of Myself" Contract

When you write a contract, the terms are apt to be specific and action-oriented. Like Elliot in the following story, you become more conscious of what you want and how to attain it.

> *Elliot prepares his papers for promotion at his job. During the last year, his company downsized and stopped the bonus program. Nevertheless, he registers for online courses with the hope of advancing to an administrative role. If you peek into the room where he works, you'll see him shuffling papers, dropping forms, misplacing reports, omitting critical dates on correspondence, and mailing invoices to the wrong vendors. But rather than face his fears, Elliot works harder and longer. He moves incessantly to ward off his worries about job security. Occasionally, he stops, looks lost in the moment, and then moves on.*

When you find yourself working harder yet realizing fewer results than you expect, it's time to ask, "Am I having a stress reaction? Could anxious feelings be undermining my productivity?"

It isn't a dishonor to experience stress during difficult times. Respect the stress. Stop to pinpoint unspoken challenges and fears. Once you understand that stress is expected, *especially* under crunch conditions, you're better prepared to manage it in a systematic, productive way.

Use Demon-Defying Strategies

Situation: You're working on an annual report for your company. You're concerned because you aren't sure about the amount you're supposed to write. The company has come up with a new design that's still in flux. You notice twice in the last few minutes you've written figures in the wrong columns. Your skin feels tight; trying to focus feels like agony.

If you want greater productivity and less stress, what can you do? At the very least, take a break and use positive self-statements to help you reduce—rather than escalate—your stress. Also adopt one or more of the following strategies.

___ *Use visualization.* First, imagine a time in the past when you felt calm and competent. Note the types of things you did when you were acting with competence and how you felt. Second, visualize a time in the future after you complete the assigned report in an accurate and timely way. See yourself smiling and comfortable. Enjoy these feelings of achievement.

___ *Use reason.* Tap into your reasoning skills to regulate your stress, mood, or anxiety using self-help guides or audios (Watson and Tharp, 2002; Hays, 2002; Johnsgard, 2004). Join community-based or hospital-based programs. Avoid falling into the habit of numbing your stress with such unhealthy options as overdrinking, overeating, overmedicating, and overusing television or computer games.

___ *Use constructive self-talk.* Give yourself permission to calm down before starting to work. For example, say, "I need to relax for a few minutes to get refreshed and regain my attention," or "I'm tired. It's all right to stop and go to bed. I'll do a better job tomorrow when I'm more alert."

___ *Use positive assertiveness.* Avoid the shame-and-blame response. Instead of saying, "I should be able to do this in one sitting," accept that multiple work sessions accompany complex, detail-oriented assignments. Create positive conditions that enable you to write a complete and accurate report.

___ *Institute a productive habit.* Get into a routine of using a stress-management strategy as soon as you become mindful of your level of stress. For example, take a few breaths, count to ten, and do stretching exercises for a few minutes. Set an alarm and take frequent short breaks to stretch and relax. Accept that when you work intensely, you expend a great deal of mental energy. Your breaks allow you to replenish that energy.

___ *Use the Stop, Look, and Listen technique.* Stop: refrain from writing for a few minutes. Look: study previous reports and any new models (even if only a few parts are already done). Look with your mind's eye and visualize both the challenges and the fears you're feeling. Listen: say calming phrases like, "I didn't create this situation, but I can find specific information to help me deal with it," or, "Perhaps I need to call a supervisor to discuss the desired format or other details of the task."

___ *Access social support.* When stressed, ask for help. Say, "Now's the time to call my friend, who helps me to regroup and get back on track."

When you call a friend or colleague, identify previous challenging times and discuss ways they were managed. Consider finding a support group for such special situations as dealing with the illness or death of a loved one. Sometimes such groups can provide the camaraderie and insight needed to get you through a highly stressful time.

Moving from Intention to Action

Although you might not avoid all stress, you can always reduce and manage it better. How? When you're in a calm state, envision what you want, why you want it, and how to get it. Give yourself time to reframe the situation and refocus on your goals, values, and past successes. Re-energize, and review your expectations and past actions. Once you become more mindful of the degree of stress you experience and the conditions surrounding it, you gain the awareness to change your reaction to stress. Doing the following exercise will help.

1. *Assess.* Visualize a work/life situation in which stress triggers distraction and inefficiency for you. Ask, "How is the Stress Demon interfering with my performance and productivity?"

_____

_____

_____

2. *Analyze consequences.* List the costs and consequences of stress-related distractions on your work/life. Ask, "As I attempt to perform my tasks, how much is stress decreasing my productivity, my image, or my self-confidence?"

_____

_____

_____

3. *Set realistic goals.* Identify one or two actions that would reduce work/life stress and enhance performance and peacefulness for you. Ask, "What are one or two doable goals to help me reduce stress and increase efficiency?"

_____

_____

_____

4. *Take action.* Identify strategies to remove or decrease your work/life stress and accompanying distractions. Ask, "When, where, and what strategies will I use to manage stress and enhance performance?" Use this chart to select and plan the strategies you're willing to use in the near future.

Stress-Management Strategies

Strategy	When and Where to Begin Using It?	Desired Outcome?	How to Monitor?
Exercise			
Humor			
Relaxation			
Rest/Break			
Yoga			
Meditation			
T'ai Chi			
Music			
Nature			
Games			
Television			
Sports			
Talking			
Hobby			

Dancing/singing			
Swimming, bathing, hot tub			
Painting, crafts			
Other			

5. *Monitor and maintain progress.* Keeping close track of your progress makes it easier to notice small improvements in your mood and/or your productivity. Ask, "How will I track my progress and reward myself? How can I deal with the barriers I see? What resources or experts might I contact for information and support?" This chart gives you a way to record your progress.

Monitoring Actions Against the Stress Demon

	Work	Home	Other
Become aware of your top stress triggers.			
Make a commitment to employ stress-management strategies in a consistent way.			
Maintain the use of currently successful stress relievers (busters).			
Identify one or two new stress-management strategies.			
Consider seeking expert advice if you constantly feel overwhelmed, sad, or stressed.			
Other			

It doesn't matter what form of stress management you use; it only matters that you find strategies that work for you. Then use those strategies consistently in your work/life settings to feel less stressed and more attentive. Bottom line: You'll have better memory and organization.

An Attorney's Stress Success Story

Harvey Kulawitz, an attorney, provides an interesting example of one professional's way of managing his job-related stress (2008). He reported,

"Riffing on a keyboard in my office helps me manage the stress of my legal practice and bond with my clients." Given the adversarial situations in his practice, he's likely to play his keyboard after a difficult phone call. Sometimes, he listens to jazz or blues. At other times, he plays for his clients.

In this case, a hobby—a positive distraction—functions as an unorthodox but workable stress reducer. It's your turn to experiment with using positive distractions to provide stress relief during your most challenging days.

THE FATIGUE DEMON

The Fatigue Demon saps the energy needed to focus and maintain concentration. Though we try to deny it, exhaustion leaves us spinning our wheels, committing errors, or even causing accidents.

9

Actions Against the Fatigue Demon

Tired from the day's activities, Burt doesn't feel like changing his loafers before climbing onto the roof to dislodge his son's kite. He overlooks the well-known hazards of climbing ladders while wearing shoes without tread. Unfortunately, he slips, falls, and smashes his foot on the cement. He requires several operations and months of physical therapy. He laments, "I was tired and impatient. This was only going to take a minute."

Burt's accident illustrates how fatigue contributes to accidents at home … and at work. As an example, fatigue accounts for high numbers of crashes and fatalities for workers who drive commercially. In addition, fatigue wreaks havoc in the lives of workers with extended hours or nontraditional or rotating work schedules. The data reported in a *Monitor on Psychology* article underscores high rates of stress, illness, accidents, and irritability when workers are overly tired (Price, 2011).

Fifty to seventy million Americans live tired lives, fatigued from lack of sleep or the day's activities, according to a Center for Disease Control (CDC) article, "Sleep Deprivation Affects a Third of Americans," on Huffington Post (Stobbe, 2011). Well over half of those surveyed reported they didn't sleep enough within the last month, and between thirty to fifty million reported having sleep disorders.

These and other studies reveal the staggering costs and consequences of sleep-related problems, especially the negative effect on attention, memory, mood, productivity—and safety. Recent research also calculates the costs of loss of workplace productivity due to poor sleep. In a survey of forty-two hundred workers in four United States corporations, fatigue-related productivity losses were estimated at an annual average cost of $1,967 per employee. For employees suffering from insomnia, the cost rises to more than $3,000; the costs to the four companies totaled fifty million dollars a year (Rosekind et al., 2010).

This chapter provides charts, checklists, and tips to help you create a Plan of Attack against distractions resulting from fatigue, distractions that diminish attention, motivation, and organization. Specifically, it discusses issues related to driving, organization, learning, irritability, and motivation.

The Fight against the Fatigue Demon

People today have busier, more hectic lives than ever before. As one person said on a radio program, "My forty-hour work week turned into a twenty-four/seven job." When that happens, the person deals with more activity, more stress, and less sleep than before.

In the short term, most people can survive on less than the recommended seven or eight hours of sleep. Over the long term, however, if you don't get the sleep you need, you're more vulnerable to distractions. Too many Americans sleep fewer than six hours a night. That's when the Fatigue Demon opens the door and invites in the Technology, Stress, and *Others* Demons. When these demons gang up, you won't have the energy to impose the discipline you need. You're apt to overeat, overuse technology, or fall into self-destructive activities like drinking excessive alcohol. You might even let others infringe on your rights. Fatigued and seeking relaxation, you can easily lose yourself to a computer game for several hours. Technology turns night into day and elevates your fatigue level—often without your awareness.

Even before the current blitz of technology-related communication, there were reports of its impact. For example, according to a National Sleep Foundation survey, about 43 percent of respondents reported staying up too late doing household chores, 33 percent on the computer or Internet, and 90 percent watching television, text messaging, or surfing the Internet (http://www.cellular-news.com/story/48194.php) (Zee, 2008).

Constant fatigue can be a symptom of such illnesses as pneumonia, anemia, diabetes, thyroid disease, or sleep apnea. In addition, poor sleep can result from stress, anxiety, hormone imbalance, or depression or other form of mental illness. In some cases, constant tiredness indicates chronic fatigue syndrome—a term that applies to those who suffer symptoms of extreme fatigue, even after rest, for at least six months. With this disease, a variety of other symptoms might come and go, including poor memory and concentration, joint pain, and headaches.

If you feel constantly tired even after receiving ample sleep, monitor when and how often you are fatigued and then discuss the situation with your health-care provider. In the following assessment, fill in the blank spaces with an *R* for rarely, an *S* for sometimes, or an *O* for often.

Self-Check: How Much and How Well Do You Sleep?

____ 1. I regularly get six to eight hours of sleep.

____ 2. I experience difficulty falling asleep.

____ 3. I am a restless sleeper, dreaming or awakening often during the night.

____ 4. I rarely feel rested and refreshed when I awake.

____ 5. I might ignore safety precautions when I am tired and inattentive.

____ 6. I don't take the time to put things away when I'm tired.

____ 7. I have trouble falling back to sleep if I wake in the middle of the night.

If you checked more than a few statements, you're probably experiencing undue fatigue and vulnerability to distraction. No one—even the strongest or toughest—is exempt from the evils of fatigue. As Vince Lombardi, the legendary football coach, said, "Fatigue makes cowards of us all."

General Consequences of the Fatigue Demon

When fatigued, the rate you're able to process information and react to events slows. You have less cognitive energy for attending to detail and thinking creatively. Nowhere does the resulting lack of attention to detail have greater consequences than when it comes to safety. For example, the US National Transportation Safety Board has found that fatigue played a role in several airplane accidents. As a result, federal agencies are charged with requiring longer rest periods for pilots.

In the medical field, residents commonly work multiple twenty-four-hour shifts in a month. Researchers found that for those with that kind of schedule, the risk of harming a patient increased by 700 percent. In response to such studies, leaders in the medical profession admitted that such practices are unsafe, discussed in a *Science News* article titled "It's time to reform work hours for resident physicians" (Czeisler, 2006, 2009).

Regardless of their field of endeavor, for most individuals the health consequences of insufficient sleep can include poor blood sugar regulation, high blood pressure, obesity, depression, irregular hormone production, and a weakened immune system. As Monica's story shows, even when you're mindful of your fatigue vulnerabilities, you might not listen to your inner voice.

Like Pinocchio's Jiminy Cricket, Monica has an inner voice that warns her, "You're tired. Don't do any more credit card charges on the virtual *terminal. Just go to bed—now!" But based on her "I'm smart, I can do anything" attitude instead of her intuition, she decides to "just do this last one." After she clicks the Send command, a bold red alert greets her: YOUR TRANSACTION IS DECLINED. Of course the charge is rejected; she posted a $95.00 charge as $9,500.00. Oops! The lesson: When your Jiminy Cricket speaks to you, listen; don't do detailed work late at night when you are fatigued.*

Fatigue has an insidious effect on organization and learning. When you feel tired, you're less organized than normal. For example, at the end of the day, lack of motivation may stifle your effort to file papers or complete chores, especially if you consider them mundane or boring. It just takes too much effort. Often, the result is disorganization—piles of mail, undone dishes, unreturned calls. You drift into the habit of *I'll do it later.*

How frequently do you notice you need to stop working because you can no longer focus and concentrate? And once you stop working, do you realize you're exhausted? Unfortunately, by the time you realize it, your work has already deteriorated. Then additional time is required to correct omissions and inaccuracies. In essence, due to the effects of fatigue, you may work twice as long with only half the result. This is especially true when you're reading or engaged in other analytical or information-processing activities.

Remember, sleep enables learning, and learning is critical in today's work world. Whether you're employed, unemployed, or under-employed, modern-day society requires that you engage in lifelong learning. Some researchers conclude that many jobs require sufficient energy to learn complicated tasks and remember how to do these tasks later (University of Chicago, 2008). Although this study involved college students, it is an important finding for non-student adults too. Research indicates a significant income gap between those with and without college or graduate work. When the economy takes a nosedive, college enrollments and online registrations soar (Sloan Survey, 2010). Many adult students see education as a way to expand or learn new skills and progress in the competitive workforce. If you need to learn, remember, and solve problems, don't expect to get great results unless you feel rested and alert.

The Consequences of Driving under the Influence—of Fatigue

While driving your car after a long day, your vision blurs; you lose focus for a split second. You take a deep breath and murmur a word of thanks because "the worst" didn't happen. You imagine killing someone by drifting into the next lane or plowing into an unsuspecting pedestrian.

Unfortunately, "the worst" happens more often than you think. While you might be aware of the dangers of driving and drinking, you might not realize that driving when drowsy can be just as dangerous—even fatal.

National statistics tell the sad story. The National Highway Transportation Safety Administration (NHTSA) estimates one hundred thousand drowsy-driving crashes are reported to police each year. In 2005, they resulted in fifteen hundred deaths and seventy-one thousand injuries, with a cost of twelve and one-half billion dollars (National Sleep Foundation, 2011). When the AAA Foundation for Traffic Safety conducted a study, it found that drivers aged sixteen to twenty-four were almost twice as likely to be involved in drowsy-driving crashes as drivers in the forty- to fifty-nine-year-old age range.

The multiple effects of fatigue while engaged in other activities apply to drowsy drivers.

- Slower reaction time. It takes the driver more time to react in an emergency.

- Reduced vigilance. The driver is slow to notice such oncoming hazards as railway crossings.

- Impaired thinking and memory. The driver might not be able to figure out what to do, might misjudge the seriousness of a situation, and/or fail to remember directions.

Assess: Sleep Thieves and Routines

Sometimes the factors that keep you from getting adequate sleep are out of your control. For example, new parents go through a period of sleep deprivation because their infant doesn't sleep through the night. However, at times other demons collude and negate your best intentions to get an adequate amount of sleep. Like a sleep thief, the Technology Demon interferes when people check e-mails in bed or leave their e-mail alert device on all night. The *Others* Demon might contact you when you need to get ready for bed or interrupt your sleep early in the morning.

What about you? Take a close look at what contributes to your fatigue. What robs you of sleep? Do you wake up in the morning more tired than when you went to sleep? Which of the following activities divert you from getting the sleep you need?

____ 1. Watching television and falling asleep in a chair with the lights on, awakening with frozen feet, a crick in your neck, and an aching back

____ 2. Playing video games, gambling online, doing social networking, or surfing the Internet

___ 3. Reading books or listening to or playing music

___ 4. Worrying about financial, social, or family problems

___ 5. Snoring or sleep apnea (or the snoring of others)

___ 6. Not sleeping due to frequent urination, hormonal disturbances, or medication effects

___ 7. Parenting or caregiving interrupting your sleep

___ 8. Job-related swing shifts or sleep interruptions due to another's work schedule

___ 9. Engaging in socializing, such as partying or card playing, late into the night

___ 10. Allowing others to interfere with falling sleep or interrupting you once you're asleep

If you want to improve your sleep behavior, take this step: collect information on your current sleep patterns and then review the ways you battle the Fatigue Demon. Use the following Weekly Sleep Journal to collect information on your sleep behavior.

Weekly Sleep Journal

Day	Hour to Begin My Sleep Routine	Sleep Routine Activities	Number of Times I Woke during the Night	Time I Arose in the Morning and How Rested I Felt	Results
1					
2					

3				
4				
5				
6				
7				

The sabotaging effect of fatigue on performance stems from your lack of awareness. You underestimate or deny the subtle, pervasive, and negative influences of fatigue on your productivity, mood, motivation, or interaction with others. To become mindful, ask and answer the following questions:

- When, where, and how is fatigue negatively affecting my attention, organization, memory, or mood?

_____

_____

- When fatigued, do I engage in such self-defeating behaviors as overeating or under-eating, excessive smoking, drinking, gaming, or overusing technology before bedtime?

  _____

  _____

- What am I doing to improve my rest and sleep? In what ways are these actions working? How do I feel about the situation?

  _____

  _____

- How serious are the fatigue-related distractions you've identified when you're at work, at home, or elsewhere? Use a scale from one to ten, with ten indicating the most serious.

Work	1	2	3	4	5	6	7	8	9	10
Home	1	2	3	4	5	6	7	8	9	10
Other	1	2	3	4	5	6	7	8	9	10

  _____

  _____

When you become more conscious of your sleep behavior, you also become better prepared to improve your sleep habits. Bottom line: you'll reduce your vulnerability to the Fatigue Demon.

Personal Consequences of Fatigue

The father of modern medicine, Hippocrates, described the negative consequences of not getting enough sleep around four hundred BC when he warned, "Insomnolency is connected with sorrow and pains."

In what ways are you *pained* due to inadequate sleep? When it comes to performance, you can be sure of one thing. When fatigue interferes with attention, the chances of poor performance increase for most people. Is that true for you? To find out, on the following list of possible negative effects of fatigue, check all that apply to you.

____ Making errors or omissions because you fail to notice important details

____ Feeling irritable, impatient, or overwhelmed

____ Spinning your wheels and accomplishing little

___ Experiencing near-accidents due to drowsiness when driving or during other activities

___ Noticing a decline in your social relationships

___ Realizing a waning interest in sex

___ Experiencing frequent forgetfulness

If you checked more than two items, it's time to make a Plan of Attack for improving your sleep habits. If symptoms are severe, contact your health provider.

Set Realistic Goals to Fight Fatigue

Setting small, simple goals facilitates your progress with any behavior change. Consider using at least one of these goals within the next week.

- Take short breaks to rest and re-energize throughout your day.

- Set an alarm to alert you to stop working at a reasonable hour at least three evenings a week and then get ready for bed.

In general, the same goals and strategies that help relieve stress also reduce fatigue. These include healthy drinks or snacks, humor, music, spirituality, and positive interaction with others. Turn to them during your downtime rather than intensely focusing on hobbies or games to move you toward greater relaxation and deeper sleep.

Be constantly mindful of ways fatigue reduces your work/life effectiveness. Visualize the next week's activities and write a simple goal to help defeat the Fatigue Demon in the coming days.

Possible goal: _____

Major Strategy: Consider a Contract

The more ingrained your unproductive sleep habits are, the more difficult they are to change. In general, fatigue undermines motivation. At bedtime when you're tired, you don't feel like changing your routine; it feels familiar, comfortable—especially at that moment. In the morning, you might feel angry or frustrated over the sluggishness you feel, but you don't break out of your negative sleep routine at night.

Because lack of energy to change is so pervasive, consider changing your habitual behavior at a slow rate. For example, attempt to go to bed earlier one or two days a week, perhaps on a Sunday night, so you get a good start on the workweek. Even if you institute a new routine for only one day a week, you'll feel a greater sense of control and optimism.

As noted earlier, an *all-or-none* approach to change is usually the least effective, especially with such habits as unproductive sleep routines. Often, you benefit from the structure that a contract can provide.

As an example, Frank has been building model ships long into the night. He's feeling crummy, so he created a contract for change with himself.

Frank's Contract for a Better Bedtime Routine

Goal: To increase the number of hours of restful sleep

Time: From 11:30 p.m. to 7 a.m. daily

Expected outcome/benefit: Feel more rested and attentive and less irritable, especially in the late afternoon

New routine: Set two alarms, one at 9:45 p.m. and one at 10 p.m. The first one reminds me to stop building and to take fifteen minutes for cleanup. The second reminds me to leave the basement *now!* Next, I take a bath, get into bed, read a hobby magazine for a few minutes, and then put on relaxing music.

Barriers: Text messaging or checking sports events

Strategies: Request that no one call or message after 10 p.m. Lower the volume of the ringer, screen calls, and only answer a call if it's an emergency.

Progress indicator: Keep a small calendar by the bed. For each night that I sleep for between seven and eight hours, draw a check mark or smiley face on the box for that day.

Issue and Strategies: Energy Drinks

Waiting in line at the Dollar Store, Geri overhears a conversation between the cashier and a shabbily dressed fourteen-year-old who is cradling a dozen brightly colored 5-Hour Energy drinks. "Sorry, you can't purchase these unless you're over eighteen," declares the cashier. The male adolescent stomps away, only to return a minute or two later with an eighteen-year-old who doles out the cash. The cashier refuses to allow the younger teen to walk out of the store with the bag. She tells the boys that the store's video cameras register every sale. The older teen angrily grabs the bag and walks out with it. What was their plan? One can only guess.

As the pace of living has increased, adolescents and young adults have turned to high-energy drinks to boost their energy and battle fatigue. Drinks such as Red Bull, Rockstar, Monster, and Full Throttle contain large amounts of caffeine and other stimulants, providing a short-term energy boost. A pint of an energy drink typically contains a cup and a half of sugar and the amount of caffeine found in four or more colas. The overuse of such drinks can be especially dangerous to those with ADHD, diabetes, epilepsy, sleep issues, and eating disorders (Neuman, 2009). Caffeine increases heart rate, and overconsumption can lead to dehydration, nervousness, irritability, and insomnia.

Some reports warn parents about the dangers of these energy drinks, and although the research isn't definitive, fatalities are linked to them. Pay attention to a serious recent trend to mix energy drinks with alcohol. Due to a powerful combination of ingredients, drinkers might be unaware that they're drunk. This leads to even more drinking and possibly dangerous incidents while driving.

If you find that you or others rely on energy drinks to stay alert and be productive, it's time to review the basics. In the short term, anyone can get away with overnighters and less sleep. But in the long run, to be mentally alert and productive, the body needs rest, exercise, and peace of mind. The occasional use of an energizing drink should not drift into an "I can't function without it" addiction. A good night's sleep coupled with good nutrition are the most positive energizers.

Issue and Strategies: Sliding into Slumber

You might describe yourself in any of the following ways: "I'm a night person; I know I work best after 9 p.m." Or "I'm a morning person; I always work best earlier in the day." Regardless of your particular sleep/wake pattern, new habits can expand the effects of your natural style, making it easy to develop a better way to slide into slumber.

The American Sleep Association advocates good sleep hygiene that includes sleeping in a quiet, comfortable, dark bedroom without interruption or noise from radios, televisions, cell phones, or other digital gadgets.

How can you improve the conditions in which you sleep? Here are various sleep products that can help you develop good sleep hygiene (Salemi, 2008). Check all that you'd consider trying within the next week or so.

_____ Noise-canceling headphones—great for those who are sensitive to noise or who travel on airplanes or commute on railroads

_____ Sleep mask—useful for those who need to sleep during the day and/or whose partners read in bed

_____ Relaxation music or audio book—to get your mind off your worries. Experiment to discover the type of music or book works best for you

___ Fans—to provide white noise

___ Aromatherapy or herbal pillows—provide pleasant aromas, such as jasmine or chamomile, to help you unwind

___ Sunset clocks—automatically and gradually dim the light to replicate the natural light cycle

Experiment to find the right strategy or combination for you.

When in the hospital, Bess, an avid reader, found that she didn't have the patience to read before going to sleep. Before her surgery, reading was a dependable way for her to unwind. Instead, she tried listening to music to relax, but it didn't work very well. Finally, she discovered that audio books invited the snoozing she needed. It was especially useful when nursing personnel interrupted her sleep during nighttime rounds. Back home she suffered from night sweats, and she relied on the audio books to lull her back to sleep.

For some, audio books would be useless for inducing sleep. However, under special circumstances, such as an illness or during high-stress periods, be open to experimenting with new techniques. You never know what will work for you.

Sometimes your thoughts keep you from restful sleep. Therefore, try to institute stress management or relaxation techniques in the evening. Try relaxing music, deep breathing, positive images, pleasant photos—whatever appeals to you. On occasion, write your worries on a sheet of paper. In most likelihood, you can't resolve the issues at this moment in time, and that's okay. Just get the thoughts out of your head and onto paper. Then plan a time when you can talk about or resolve the dilemmas. If stress interferes with sleep on an ongoing basis, consult a health-care or mental health professional.

Issue and Strategies: Managing Morning Malaise

For many who don't consider themselves *morning people*, getting up early is arduous. They turn off the alarm (if they hear it), feel groggy, take too long to shower and dress, and waste time getting out of the house. Frequently, they arrive at work or an appointment late and forget to bring the items they need. This problem can be especially acute for those working from home or having unstructured jobs. As a result, they fall into a low rate of task completion, feel inadequate, and subsequently lose their momentum.

All is not lost. You can employ strategies to stop fatigue from holding you back. Go to sleep earlier, set more than one alarm, and ask others to make sure that you rise at a healthy time if necessary. (Too much sleep is reported to intensify feelings of sadness and inertia.) If working at home, get up and get dressed as if you were going to an office. This creates the routine of *work time*. Sometimes, you need to get started by getting out of the house. Perhaps go to a coffee shop or gym. Use the time to become alert and energized. While in a coffee shop, decide on or review your daily goals and then modify your schedule. If you can't work in a busy place, go to a local library.

> *Scott, a creative mechanical type, tinkers until the wee hours and is a mess in the mornings. His tardiness and irritability are "downers" to all attending the morning staff meetings. Not surprisingly, the staff begin to arrive later and later to the meetings. Eventually Scott's fatigue-related behavior will negatively affect the bottom line. His partner complains and pressures Scott to change. Using logic, Scott accepts the fact that he doesn't have the right to drag the business down because of his particular sleep habits. He agrees that he needs to take action. So his plan is to set three alarms. One alarm will signal him to stop working at night. In the morning, he'll set two other alarms fifteen minutes apart at different locations in his bedroom. The result? For four days a week, he arrives at the office on time, alert and ready to interact positively with his staff. When working at home on innovations and special projects, he sleeps late and enjoys greater time flexibility.*

Unproductive morning habits are difficult to change. In this case, Scott bolsters his efforts by using alarms. It takes two or three weeks to make a change, but once he puts his new habit in place, he won't need as many supports.

Use Demon-Defying Strategies

Situation: It's late, and you're feeling pressured to complete your tax return. You misplace receipts. You need to redo figures. Even using a calculator, your head pounds. If you want greater productivity, what can you say or do?

____ *Use visualization.* Visualize the possible positive and negative consequences. See your tax refund greatly reduced because your paperwork wasn't complete and accurate. Next, imagine the lovely things you could do with the money if you get a substantial refund.

____ *Use reason.* You know the seriousness of income tax returns. Say, "If I make mistakes, it may cost me. If I'm really inaccurate, red flags could even trigger an audit."

____ *Engage in constructive self-talk.* Do you need to give yourself a pep talk to increase the frequency of positive behaviors? If someone cared about you, what would he or she say to help you? What message can you tell yourself to spur healthier sleep habits? Give yourself permission to work when you are more alert. For example, say, "My head is pounding, and I'm wasting time. I'll finish it tomorrow when I can do a better job; it'll go faster."

___ *Use positive assertiveness.* Remember your responsibility to establish productive work conditions. Perhaps when your work requires detail and accuracy, you need to reschedule to another time. Say, "It doesn't make sense for me to work when I'm so exhausted. When I'm alert, I'll do this in half the time and with fewer mistakes."

___ *Institute productive habits.* Be creative, and find ways to check your work. One accountant checks her accuracy and completeness on each section after a break, when she has a fresh eye for details.

___ *Stop, Look, and Listen technique.* Stop. Engage in productive self-talk and logic by saying, "This is ridiculous. I'm too tired to pay attention." Look at work you accomplished when you were alert and compare it to this. Listen to your good sense and say, "I must stop and take a break or work on this another time."

___ *Access social support.* Contact a trusted person and share your feelings about this tedious job. Make a date to work side by side. Like young children who engage in parallel play (playing on their own in the midst of other children), schedule periods for *parallel work.* Set a doable schedule of twenty- to thirty-minute periods with short breaks. It's surprising how much better you stay on task and get things done when working with another.

If sleep problems continue, consider contacting your physician or a hospital-based sleep clinic. Discover what the experts know about fatigue problems and solutions, particularly if you experience chronic insomnia, bad dreams, nightmares, and/or night terrors.

Moving from Intention to Action

1. *Assess.* Review your self-checks and journals or diaries. Visualize some work/ life situation during which your productivity lags due to fatigue. Ask, "How is the Fatigue Demon interfering with my attention, productivity, or safety?"

_____

_____

2. *Analyze consequences.* Does it make sense to be the one who creates obstacles to your performance and sense of well-being? Think about the time, money, or safety precautions you ignore due to fatigue-related distractions. Ask, "As I attempt to meet work/life responsibilities, in what ways and to what degree do fatigue-related distractions interfere with my productivity and safety?"

_____

_____

3 *Set realistic goals.* Identify one or two ways you can change work/life conditions and consequences to improve rest and increase productivity or safety. Ask, "What are one or two doable ways to increase my attention to important activities? What positive outcomes could result from setting these goals?"

_____

_____

4. *Take action.* List strategies to remove or decrease your work/life fatigue-related distractions so you can achieve your goals. Ask, "What strategies will I try? When and where?"

_____

_____

5. *Monitor and maintain progress.* Developing new sleep routines is not easy. By monitoring your progress, you discover which strategies to continue and how to modify your plan when things don't progress as you'd like. Ask, "How will I keep track of progress toward my goals? What rewards can I access to sustain my motivation? What pitfalls or other demons might interfere with my plan? How will I meet these challenges?"

Monitoring Actions Against the Fatigue Demon

	Work	**Home**	**Other**
Be honest when assessing the amount of restful, uninterrupted sleep you get and any resulting feelings of fatigue.			
Become aware of your energy cycle. When does fatigue hamper learning, productivity, or social interactions?			

Make a commitment to impose a healthy sleep routine.			
Identify aids or techniques to follow your healthy sleep routine.			
Consider the use of naps or rest times.			
Consider seeking the advice of an expert if you constantly feel tired, especially if you're getting adequate rest.			

Remember, if you're one of the 10 percent of Americans who suffer from chronic insomnia, you may benefit from working with a hospital- or community-based psychologist. For example, studies have shown using cognitive behavior therapy can be as effective as sleeping pills. Plus such therapies are useful for other sleep-related conditions, including sleep apnea, restless leg syndrome, and shift-work difficulties (Jacobs, 2004).

Sheila's Fatigue Success Story

Recently, I had several errands to run, so to help me stay focused, I made a list. In addition to the list, I pictured my route and numbered the spots in the order I would stop—all within a mile stretch. First, I went to the bank and made my deposit. Next, I went to the tailor to have a pair of pants hemmed. At Stop #3 to return an item I'd purchased earlier, I gathered my stuff from the car, locked the door with the remote key control, and began walking into the store. Suddenly, I realized I didn't have my purse, where I'd put the receipt. I figured I'd left it in the car, so I went back to fetch it. It wasn't there! Momentary panic set in—and then I remembered I had set it down in the fitting room when I tried on my pants. Forgetting my purse was unusual and a little scary. Naturally, I quickly drove back to the tailor. However, in a neighborhood I know well, I drove right past his driveway! I was able to make the next turn and navigate back to the correct building, but I thought, What's going on? I never do this. Am I going nuts?

Then it hit me: I was being attacked by the Fatigue Demon! I went to sleep late and got up early. I didn't eat lunch and was basically distracted. It felt so good to be able to name what was going on! Recognizing my demon made me feel relieved and in control of the situation. I would soon be able to head home and take a nap.

I realized that by preparing my errand list ahead of time, I caught my error (no receipt, no purse) immediately and could retrace my steps quickly and logically. Next time, I can add a checklist to my errand list to make sure I have everything after each stop. I could also carry a snack in the car to recharge my energy between errands. All in all, I know I'm on the right track in managing this better!

For Sheila, awareness is a key factor. By understanding the reason for her "spacey" behavior, she stops the blaming and shaming. Instead, she moves into a logical, positive problem-solving mode. She selects an appropriate strategy (taking a nap) and puts in place a preventative measure for next time—carrying energizing snacks.

Actions Against the Illness/ Medication Demon

Married for fifteen years, a psychologist and a physician joke while they unpack the supplies for Sally's colonoscopy. "I hate the taste of this stuff!" says Sally about the concoction she has to take the day before the procedure. Loren laughs. "Just chug-a-lug and you'll be okay." She survives the night and awakens feeling starved. She grabs a granola bar as she rushes off to the doctor's office. Just before going in for the procedure, the nurse asks her, "Sally, you haven't eaten anything in the last twelve hours, have you?" Oops! A Demon of Distraction just attacked.

While joking around the night before the test, neither of these highly educated persons paid attention to the directions at the top of the instruction page. As a consequence of her inattention, there's no test for Sally that day. She needs to go through the preparation again and lose another personal day from work.

If you've experienced an examination like Sally's, you know it requires arduous preparation. You drink gallons of a prepared potion and make unending trips to the bathroom, often throughout the night. Although Sally and Loren are experienced with medical tests, they were both distracted. The lesson for all of us is to take a quiet minute to pay attention to any pre-procedural instructions.

When you are ill, have chronic health problems, and/or take medications, you can become especially vulnerable to distraction. Even subtle side effects of medication or anesthesia can result in lack of concentration, memory loss, or fatigue. Like Sally, you experience a variety of inconveniences, including the loss of work time and money. In addition, inconvenience can trigger irritation and stress, which increases your vulnerability to even more distraction and annoyance.

This chapter provides you with charts, checklists, and tips to make a Plan of Attack against distractions associated with illness and/or medication. It addresses issues that include medication side effects, medical incidents, headaches, surgery, and cancer.

Interference by the Illness/Medication Demon

Illness and medication are intertwined within this demon. Jeff suffers from chronic headaches and arthritis and takes quantities of aspirin, plus a nonsteroidal anti-inflammatory drug like ibuprofen to treat the pain and inflammation. However, too many of these over-the-counter remedies can cause stomach irritation. Unaware of possible side effects, Jeff suffered serious consequences; the drug created excess acidity that led to a bleeding ulcer, which was discovered only when he was rushed to the emergency room.

Americans spent more than 307 *billion* dollars on prescription medications in 2010 (Gatyas, 2011). Some reports label the United States as the country with the highest number of medicated citizens in the world. According to one government report, almost half of all insured Americans took at least one prescription drug in a month; more than 40 percent of older Americans took five or more prescription drugs (Gu, 2010).

Once you start taking medication, you need to monitor your reactions to them. Say you go to several different physicians and fill prescriptions to deal with different health problems. Does one doctor know what the other prescribes? How well do the different medications work when taken together? Beware: the combinations can be dangerous. In an article titled "When Mixing Medications Can Be Deadly," one expert says, "People are often woefully unaware of the potentially serious consequence of the additive effects of [mixing] prescription medications" (Wang, 2008).

Also be aware of the potential abuse of prescription drugs. State and federal governments attempt to alert the public with such articles as "Legal Drugs Kill Far More than Illegal, Florida Says" (Cave, 2008). Plus, the use of a prescription medication for nonmedical reasons is on the rise in the United States across all age groups. National studies (reported in 2004 by National Institute on Drug Abuse, or NIDA) note that approximately 20 percent of those in the United States population have used prescription drugs for nonmedical reasons in their lifetime (NIDA). The most commonly abused medications are such strong narcotic painkillers as OxyContin or Vicodin, as well as stimulant medications prescribed for ADHD. In fact, the FDA is stepping up its efforts to reduce unsafe use of narcotic products, such as methadone pills, Fentanyl patches, extended-release pills containing morphine, and other sedative narcotics (Rubin, 2009). That tells you to stay alert. Whether prescription or nonprescription, it's easier than you think to fall into a habit of overusing (or abusing) drugs.

When you have an illness and take medication, distractions can be frequent because your focus, memory, or other thinking functions can be affected. In addition, you can experience a variety of physical side effects. Use the following checklist to note any side effects you experience frequently.

Self-Check: Frequently Experienced Side Effects

____ 1. Memory loss

____ 2. Headaches

____ 3. Heartburn or gastrointestinal distress

____ 4. Upper respiratory problems

____ 5. Aches and pains

____ 6. Lack of concentration

____ 7. Irritability or mood change

____ 8. Lower gastrointestinal distress

____ 9. Jitters

____ 10. Rash or hives

If you experience frequent side effects, contact your medical care provider. Call or e-mail to check about any persistent symptoms you may refer to as "no big deal." Let the professionals decide whether they need attention or not.

General Consequences: Illness and Lifestyle

Within the general population, the leading causes of death are heart disease and cancer (Center for Disease Control, 2007). Today's health literature espouses the benefits of healthy lifestyle choices, including stress management for preventing these common diseases.

People, however, don't easily change their behaviors. In fact, the US population is experiencing an alarming increase in poor lifestyle choices, demonstrated by the rising rates of obesity and diabetes in children and adults. For example, according to a recent survey by the Centers for Disease Control and Prevention, "About one-third of US adults (33.8 percent) are obese, and approximately 17 percent of children and adolescents between two and nineteen years are obese" (Center for Disease Control, 2007–2008).

Without doubt, almost everyone can benefit from modifying such lifestyle factors as poor diet, physical inactivity, and overuse or abuse of tobacco, alcohol, and drugs. Does your busy life distract you from making choices that improve your own health and well-being?

Assess: Medical History

You think you're fine, but periodically you get an infection. Over the past few years, you've had abscesses in your nose, under your arm, in the groin area, and most recently, a nasty, painful infection in your lower abdomen. It seems like these incidents are unrelated, but are they?

For one patient, Zona, they weren't. After experiencing a painful crisis, Zona's laboratory results indicated an insidious staph infection. In previous years, although antibiotics seemingly cured the condition, the infection lay dormant. Perhaps keeping a log of medical incidents could have brought this situation to light earlier and prevented distress for Zona.

Too often, records about you and your family's illnesses and health-care visits go untracked or are misplaced or discarded. As the years slip by, it becomes more difficult to remember incidents and locate existing records. Physicians move, offices close, and medical records disappear. When an illness or accident occurs, it's frustrating, time consuming, and tedious to backtrack and recreate a person's medical history.

What can you do right now? Set up a simple filing system to record incidents, visits, laboratory results, vaccine dates, hospital stays, and other relevant medical history for each person in the family. If file folders are apt to be misplaced, it might be easier to store information in a three-ring binder with separate tabs for each family member. Store the business cards and brochures of health-care providers or resources in plastic sleeves or cardholders. If you like to take a record sheet to a medical appointment, file it in a notebook so you can easily access it when needed.

Ask your physician to forward reports or notes from your office visits so you have a reliable history if and when you need it. If you have several medical appointments within a brief period, keep a summary sheet of the visits. Here is a sample log for recording your critical health information.

Health Log

Name: _____ Age: _____ Starting Date: _____

Date	Health Provider	Activity: Visit, Test, or Hospital Stay	Insurance/ Costs	Follow-up or Lesson Learned

Personal Consequences of the Illness/Medication Demon

If you've had a recent medical condition, you might notice greater distractibility than usual due to your pain and discomfort. Feeling fatigued and inattentive, you might fail to notice an adverse reaction to an over-the-counter or prescription medication, perhaps an allergic reaction or stomach upset or diarrhea.

> *Despite the recent downsizing of the health-care company where she works, Rita not only gets to keep her job but also gains a promotion. Given the economic climate, however, she still worries about finances. As she begins to take on her new responsibilities, she develops a sty on her eye that won't heal. She wears dark glasses to hide the ugly swelling and inflammation. After taking an antibiotic for ten days, her eye is better, but she has flu-like symptoms, such as fatigue, aching joints, and general malaise. She says to a friend, "I just don't feel right. I think the stress from the new job is wearing me down." Her friend responds, "I don't think so. It seems more like an allergic reaction rather than stress."*

A call to Rita's physician provides the answer. She's experiencing classic signs of an adverse reaction to a sulfa-based antibiotic commonly prescribed for eye problems. Although Rita had never reacted adversely to any other antibiotic, she did to this one. Eager to use the medication, she neglected to read the information attached to the prescription package.

You've heard this simple advice before—please don't ignore it. Always read the accompanying literature on and in boxes of over-the-counter and prescription medications. Be cautious when taking herbal remedies and supplements as well. Be on the lookout for side effects, and take the following actions if you notice any changes.

- Write notes about when, where, and for how long you experience any difficulty.

- Discuss your behavior with family and friends. Ask, "Have you noticed any changes in my behavior since I began the new medication?"

- Call your health-care provider and insist on talking to someone or going in.

- Call or visit your pharmacist to gain information.

- Look up the medication in a medical reference source and find out its properties.

Even a cold or allergy medication can cause you to act flakey and put you in an awkward situation professionally. Reactivity to medication can be especially severe for youngsters and elderly people. In fact, some antibiotics trigger extreme emotional disturbances in elderly patients.

Set Realistic Goals to Protect against the Illness/Medication Demon

Don't be distracted and miss the obvious when it comes to good health. Good habits could add years to your life. According to research, "—being physically active, not smoking, drinking alcohol only moderately and eating at least five servings of fruits and vegetables each day could extend your life by fourteen years" (Alpert, 2009).

Take a few minutes to review what lifestyle changes might decrease work/life distractions for you. In the midst of your busy life, it takes conscious effort to switch into prevention mode. Do this: look at photographs from times when you felt healthy and strong. If you need to get back on a positive track, think about the smallest goal that would help you move toward improved health. What simple goals might you consider?

Consider these lifestyle changes that might reduce the distractions fostered by the Illness/Medication Demon.

- Post a list of your medications in an accessible place.

- Review the informational material that accompanies any medication that you take.

- Join a center to learn such healthy activities as yoga, dancing, or other choice.

- Commit to engaging in recreational or exercise activities with a friend.

- Fill a plastic bag with your regular medications to be ready for emergencies, unexpected trips, or natural disasters.

To make your goals doable, write down one activity you're willing to do once a week or month at a specific time of day.

What could you say or do to avoid distractions posed by illness or medication? List them here:

- At work: _____

- At home: _____

- Other setting: _____

Major Strategy: Carry Updated Medical Information

Although Dave is relatively young, he has a heart condition and takes a variety of medications, including a beta-blocker and diuretic, plus blood pressure and cholesterol medications. In addition, he is temporarily on Coumadin, an anticoagulant. He slips and hits his head on the ice; when he loses consciousness, he is taken to the emergency room. Wouldn't it have been extremely useful if he wore a medical alert identification bracelet or carried emergency contact information and a list of current medications?

It's easy these days to store emergency contact information in your cell phone address book. Use the initials ICE: In Case of Emergency. If you have more than one emergency contact, list each as ICE1, ICE2, and so on.

Similarly, you can carry an updated medication inventory on a wallet-sized card and/or in a PDA. Spouses and significant others also need to carry your information in their address books or PDAs (and vice versa). Adult children who are caregivers for their parents often keep checklists of their parents' medications in a visible place, such as on the refrigerator or bathroom door, making that information easily available to emergency personnel. Of course, any medication inventory needs frequent updating. Here's an example.

Medication Inventory

Name: _____

Address: _____ Phone/E-mail: _____

Emergency Contacts: _____

Medication: Prescription or Over-the-Counter?	Dosage/ with or without Food?	Pharmacy and Prescription Number	Possible Side Effects	Prescribing Physician/ Contact Information	Time(s) of the Day to Take Medication
1.					
2.					
3.					
4.					
5.					

It's important to dispose of outdated medications. Follow these three steps.

1. Schedule fifteen minutes every six months to check the expiration dates for medications in your medicine chest or other storage area(s).

2. Discard any outdated prescriptions or over-the-counter medications, such as cough syrup, antihistamine, and antacid.

3. Make a list of medication or supplies to replace.

Keep all current information in an address book or on a separate sheet of paper taped to a closet door.

Issue and Strategies: Getting Ready for Surgery

The surgeon says, "You'll need to get those bunions taken care of." When you're told that a foot operation is required, you spend time making arrangements and perhaps worrying about the outcome or possible pain. These concerns could distract you and prevent you from investigating ways to effectively deal with the situation.

Don't deny or avoid addressing your worries. Schedule quiet time to consider the following possibilities and put them in priority:

- Discuss options with your physician or nurse practitioner.

- Join a support group.

- Ask a family member or friend to help you organize and prepare.

- Access online information or resource centers.

- Consider relaxation training, hypnosis, and/or acupuncture.

Make a checklist of things to take to the hospital. The closer some people get to the hospitalization date, the greater their stress—and the greater their chances of acting in a scatterbrained manner. Here's a handy checklist of items you'll want to bring to the hospital, especially for an extended stay.

___ Personal hygiene or other items, such as toothbrush, toothpaste, floss, mouthwash, baby powder, lip balm, hand lotion, deodorant, hard candies, gum, mints, or cough drops

___ Comfort items, such as a favorite pillow or comforter, robe or sweater, photos, and even stuffed animals

___ General supplies, such a small spiral book with a pen attached to note information, a small clock with a lighted face, and small white board with dry erase marker

___ Entertainment or business items, including mobile phone, iPod, transistor radio, DVD player, playing cards, chargers or batteries, and candy for visitors or hospital staff.

Have a family member check on how to securely store your personal items when you're in surgery or therapy so you don't experience any mysterious disappearances.

Realize that when you're in the hospital, your memory and organizational skills could falter. If you're there for an extended period, use such aids as notebooks, signs, and whiteboards.

> *Joel had a serious injury and was sedated. His family used a white board and dry erase marker to keep track of visitors and communicate with them. This served to alert family and friends about what not to give the patient and also to pose questions for medical and other professional staff.*

If you've gone though long hospitalizations involving family or friends, you've learned about the need to have creature comforts on hand, not only for the patient but for the family.

> *Waiting for days to learn about the extent of a serious accident, out-of-town family members spent countless hours in waiting rooms. One late night, two relatives felt especially alone and frightened. Wrapped in hospital blankets, they cried, sipped a bit of bourbon from paper cups, and nibbled on Hershey Kisses. These creature comforts helped them get through. They discovered the value of social support the next day when a gift box with a coffee cake arrived from Zingerman's, a hometown deli. The cake tasted great, but the greater gift was the rush of warmth each bite brought as they remembered their friends at home. Everyone needs care during a medical crisis.*

Issue and Strategies: Cancer

Cancer is the second-leading cause of death in the United States (Hoyert and Xu, 2012). This disease fosters physical and mental strains on the patient and family alike. Tests, waiting time for diagnosis, office visits, and treatments trigger a host of distractions. Regardless of how smart or competent you are, you will benefit from systematic ways of monitoring your medications.

Fatigue is a symptom associated with many cancer treatments. When you're tired, it's easy to get distracted and forget things. For example, you could wake from a nap and feel pain and nausea. You grab and swallow the medication you think you need and go back to sleep. Later in the day, you can't remember if you took one or two pills. When you are ill and taking numerous medications, you need to carefully keep track; have others in your family assist you.

Zach, a cancer patient, takes more medication than he ever took before. He says, "I have chemo brain!" He lives alone and decides to take action. First, he creates "Zach's Pill Diary" to keep track of when and how much medication he takes. He wants to avoid mix-ups—especially because he's taking powerful painkillers, antidepressants, and sleep medications. Second, he includes a section to track the amount of pain and possible side effects that he experiences each day. Third, he uses his habit of checking the weather to trigger his use of the pill diary. After looking at the weather report, he notes the day's weather on the top of the chart. This action brings his attention to the diary and invites him to use it. Because he feels groggy in the morning, he might otherwise forget to take the medications. In addition, using a pill diary reduces his tendency to put off taking his morning medications and helps him organize them for the rest of the day.

Sample of Zach's Pill Diary

WEEK: _____

DAY and DATE: _____ WEATHER: _____

Pain level at awakening: 1 2 3 4 5 6 7 8 9 10
Pain level after medication: 1 2 3 4 5 6 7 8 9 10

	Drugs	Opana: 10 mg	Opana: Break through	Hydro-cortisone	Warfarin: 2 mg	Prevacid: 30 mg
Times						
6 A.M.						
7 A.M.						

If you or others need to monitor medication, use a special interest like sports, entertainment, or nature to trigger your attention. This increases the chances that effective medication management becomes a reality rather than remaining a good intention.

Issue and Strategies: Chronic Illnesses

The term *chronic illness* applies to an illness that lasts for three or more months. Chronic ailments might include arthritis, asthma, diabetes, coronary heart disease, and chronic obstructive lung disease. The long-term nature of such problems can wear you down, especially if you suffer side effects from multiple medications. You get distracted with the management of the symptoms or side effects and become unaware of the subtle changes in your mood and motivation. For these reasons, keep track of your moods in a journal or calendar. If you feel burdened, sad, or angry, you may lack the *oomph* to follow the necessary medical regimen. Consequently, you won't get the nutrition or the exercise you need. You won't reach out or communicate enough. You may make poor lifestyle choices and exacerbate your medical problems.

In addition to monitoring your physical condition and feelings, create a notebook with information about your health providers, and note the results of each office visit. Here's an example of a chart you could use.

Physical and Mental Health Providers

Provider	Address	Telephone & Fax	E-mail	Login/ Password	Notes
Internist/ Primary Physician					
Dentist					
Orthodontist					
Allergist					
Psychiatrist					
Psychologist					
Social Worker					
Sleep Clinic					
Depression Center					
Physical Therapist					
Other					
Other					

Every doctor you see takes notes, and so should you. If you're not a great note-taker, then take someone with you or request that an assistant provide you with some notes. You, like Fred, might want to develop your own form.

Fred's Doctor Visit Form

Patient: _____Chart #: _____ Date: _____

Doctor: _____Specialty: _____

Purpose of visit:

_____

Significant changes, physical or mental, since last visit: _____

_____

Symptoms: _____

Findings: _____

BP: ___/___   <120/<80

Pulse: _____

Weight: _____

Temp: _____

White count: _____ normal between 4,500 and 10,000

Protime: _____   < 3 and >2

Hemoglobin A$_1$C: _____   < 7.0 percent

Urine analysis _____

Test results: _____

Prescribed: drug: _____, dosage: _____mg,

frequency: _____ (daily, twice a day, three times a day),

how long to take: _____ (rest of my life, until symptoms are

relieved, one week), correct dosage for ___ year old?

Additional tests needed: _____

Follow-up date: _____

Comments: _____

Seek a delicate balance when dealing with chronic medical issues. In most cases, focusing on healthy lifestyle habits, including adequate sleep, exercise, and stress management, helps to manage nagging health problems.

Use Demon-Defying Strategies

If you believe you're doing yourself a disservice by not engaging in healthy lifestyle behaviors, ask, "When will I *seize the day* to improve my health?" Remember that each dawn brings a new opportunity to change a habit and improve your health.

____ *Use visualization.* Evoke positive images of times when you felt energetic or healthier. Compare them to the current picture. Is there more stress, alcohol, food? Is there less sleep and exercise?

___ *Use reason.* Ponder ways you can accept the realities presented by decades of research. What is the barrier to you acting on your behalf to enhance your health and well-being? What lessons have you learned about health? What are examples of times when you used good judgment?

___ *Use constructive self-talk.* Read the statistics relative to enjoying a healthy lifestyle. Star or circle the facts or goals that relate to you. For example, regardless of age, everyone needs at least thirty minutes of exercise three or four times a week. Conduct an internal dialogue: "What are the two or three healthy activities I engage in? How often do I engage in each activity? Do I need to give myself a pep talk to increase the frequency of this positive behavior?" For example, if you plan to exercise but don't feel like it at the moment, make positive statements such as:

- I promised I would _____. Keep the commitment!

- I need to take care of myself. Start now or it won't get done.

- I'll call _____, she always gives me the boost I need.

- What else might you say? _____

___ *Use positive assertiveness.* You plan to exercise, but your friend calls and puts pressure on you to go out. You say, "I'd love to, but I promised myself that I'd go to the gym. If you want, come with me, or let's schedule another time to get together."

___ *Institute productive habits.* It doesn't seem like you're eating too much—only a spoonful of ice cream or an oversized portion of protein. But it all adds up. Rarely can exercise alone contribute to significant weight loss. Considering your health, if you need to drop some weight, then engage in a productive habit. For a few days each month, count the calories you consume and see how fast they add up. Such reality checks help you maintain a healthy weight or reduce your daily intake of calories, depending on your goal.

___ *Use the Stop, Look, and Listen technique.* You exercised and worked up a sweat. You're pleased with yourself. You decide to reward yourself with a large mucho-mocha beverage (400 calories) and a blueberry muffin (350 calories).

Stop to calculate the number of calories. Look at the recommended daily number of calories for your age and body type, and then visualize yourself stuffing your mouth with 750 extra calories. Listen to the experts you've heard who say, "If you snack, then prepare; have healthy, low-calorie drinks and foods on hand."

____ *Access social support.* At least once a week, contact a friend to schedule time to exercise or engage in a recreational activity. Join a community-based exercise program or boot camp. Plan fun, relaxing activities for at least half a day a month or for one day every season. You'll gain energy and motivation by doing so.

Although no one can avoid all accidents or illnesses, you can prevent distraction from making a bad situation worse. First, be aware of the dangers of medication and their possible side effects. Second, keep track of how much medication you take and how you feel.

Moving from Intention to Action

There is no time like the present to commit to and initiate positive action. For many, the hardest part of the move from good intention to action is the first step. Imagining a positive consequence counteracts inertia and lowers resistance to change.

1. *Assess.* Visualize health-wise activities that would help you ensure your wellness, deal with illness, or manage your medications. Review self-checks and journals. Ask, "How is the Illness/Medication Demon interfering with my productivity? Can I envision a healthier me?"

_____

_____

2. *Analyze consequences.* List the costs and consequences of distractions as they relate to illnesses, medications, or insufficient health-wise behaviors. Estimate the time, money, or energy you waste due to distractions. Ask, "As I try to complete my daily activities, to what degree is health-related distraction interfering with my productivity, diminishing my health, or wasting time or money? What positive consequences would I experience if I increased even one positive lifestyle behavior?"

_____

_____

3. *Set realistic goals.* Visualize ways that would help you move toward more positive consequences. Ask, "What are one or two goals to decrease distractions and increase my performance when engaged in important work/ life activities?"

_____

_____

4. *Take action.* Identify strategies to remove or decrease distractions at work or home. Ask, "When, where, and how will I move from intention to action? What specific strategies or tips will I use?"

You consider action but you think, "I don't know where to start. Won't it be a waste if I start and then stop?" or "I don't have the time or energy." Sometimes it helps to imagine increasing one health-wise routine. Because exercise is a frequently neglected but important health-related activity, consider increasing your amount of weekly exercise. Start small, but be consistent. For example, get aerobic exercise for fifteen, twenty, or thirty minutes, two to four times a week. Select an activity that's easy to integrate into your schedule. Common activities include walking, running, biking, swimming, calisthenics, or dancing. For some, Nintendo's Wii provides the exercise needed.

If you're not ready to commit to exercise, increase your awareness or motivation by reading a few articles, using an audio or video program, or subscribing to health or exercise newsletters. List what you're willing to do here.

_____

_____

5. *Monitor and maintain progress.* The more frequently you reward and recognize your efforts to avoid a distracting behavior, the easier it is to keep going in the right direction. Ask, "How can I deal with barriers or other demons that distracted me in the past from engaging in healthy activities? How will I track progress toward my goal? What rewards can I provide myself to sustain my motivation? What resources or experts might I contact if I have questions or need support?"

It's always difficult to get started, so begin with small steps. Here are several practical ideas to help you defeat the subtle but often negative effects of the Illness/ Medication Demon.

Monitoring Actions Against the Illness/Medication Demon

	Work	Home	Other
Increase awareness of the number and effects of medications you use.			
Make a commitment to impose healthier lifestyle routines.			
Sign a medical directive and appoint a medical guardian. Provide the location of valuables, credit cards, and medical/legal/ insurance information.			
Plan ahead and allow ample time for recuperation following elective dental or medical procedures.			
Provide others with emergency contacts in case you become incapacitated. Include names and numbers of physicians and lawyers.			
Plan regular checkups with physicians, dentists, and other medical or mental health professionals.			

Arnold's Illness/Medication Success Story

Arnold J. Gold of Connecticut shared his experience in his article "What Fitness Has Done for Me" on the website www.healthchecksystems.com/success.htm.

> *At the age of 53, I found myself having to think very seriously about my health. I was diabetic (diagnosed at the age of thirty-seven) and was taking sixty units nph insulin and a second shot of regular insulin every day. I was sixty pounds overweight and sedentary. I didn't pay attention to exercise, and my diet was very unhealthy. I ate out at restaurants too often and I was making very poor food choices. My diabetes was out of control, and I was afraid of having to face a third laser surgery for my eyes. It was time to do something."*

Arnold goes on to explain what he did. For example, he read about diet and nutrition and exercised. He used a bike to exercise and increased from two minutes, eight times a day, to forty minutes at a time. He monitored portion sizes, types, and calories of foods, and he reduced the number of times he ate in restaurants. After describing his eating routines, Arnold relates his results.

> *"After only six months of following this program, I'd lost thirty-five pounds (about one pound a week) and with my doctor's permission, I was able to discontinue my intake of insulin and take pills instead. Now five years after starting my diet and exercise program, I have maintained a seventy-pound weight loss. My waist has gone from 44 inches to 36 inches, and my cholesterol has dropped."*

He ends his story by saying, *"Living healthy has become a way of life for me. I can honestly say that by starting a fitness program, I have not only improved my life, but I may have saved my life as well."*

Triggered by a medical crisis, Arnold manages his Illness Demon through diet, exercise, and general fitness information. Stories like his provide inspiration to engage in healthy behaviors and avoid negative consequences associated with the Illness/Medication Demon.

The Unruly Mind Demon can have three heads.
It can involve a racing mind, daydreaming, or hyper focus.
The more unruly the mind, the less productive we are.

11

Actions Against the Unruly-Mind Demon

Keith, his wife Eleanor, and a staff member rush to Costco to buy groceries for the Fourth of July office party. The creative human resources manager of a small computer company, Keith usually has more ideas than he can reasonably carry out in a brief period. In fact, before he finishes one task, he thinks of the next.

He moves fast, joking all the while. Amid gales of laughter, he and the team fly through the aisles, filling their carts with cases of beer, soda, and food. "No problem; we'll be in and out in a flash," brags Keith. Gulping Cokes, the team sighs with satisfaction as they push the carts out of the store. Suddenly, Keith realizes that instead of bringing the company van, he'd brought his compact car. "Oops!" There they stand in the humid, hot parking lot, waiting for more than an hour until the secretary arrives with the van.

Keith has so many ideas racing through his mind that he fails to think ahead. His thoughts scattered, he acts more on impulse than on logic. His story illustrates one type of the Unruly-Mind Demon—racing thoughts. Another type involves inappropriate hyper-focus, which happens when you're unable to tear yourself away from a project or hobby. Still another kind of an unruly mind involves excessive daydreaming or mind wandering—perhaps during an important meeting or sports competition. Any one of these can seriously impede your attempts to get ahead or avoid undue stress.

As intelligent as you might be, you're vulnerable to having too many thoughts at once, drifting off with new ideas (or worries) or sticking with a task long after you cease to be effective. Like Keith, you might act impulsively when you're rushing or under pressure. These tendencies contribute to disorganization and lackluster performance and need to be curbed. It takes practice to stop debilitating habits and start paying attention to paying attention.

This chapter addresses how you can deal with three aspects of an unruly mind: hyper-focus, racing thoughts, and daydreaming. It offers strategies to reduce these tendencies, increase productivity, and decrease stress.

The Hassle of Hyper-Focus

> *At her sister's wedding, Julie gives this survival tip to the groom: "Here's a warning; don't interrupt my sister when she's on the computer. She won't respond. You'll think she's deaf. After you make many polite attempts to get her attention, you'll scream at her and perhaps stamp your feet. Finally, she'll look up, smile, and sweetly ask, "'What's the big deal?'"*

Hyper-focus is the ability to concentrate on one task to the exclusion of others. Part of a larger set of attention skills, it's extremely useful when used appropriately. Yet inappropriate hyper-focus can lead to unproductive habits and/or inconsiderate behavior. Some people work in this mode until they're exhausted, only to discover that the last pieces of their work were disjointed and useless.

Do you have a tendency to overuse your ability to hyper-focus? This checklist helps you assess your own tendency. Read each item and check all that apply to you.

Self-Check: Hyper-Focus

____ 1. Once I begin a task, I won't stop until it's completed.

____ 2. I have a difficult time beginning tasks, but once I start, I ignore everything else.

____ 3. I keep working on something for too long; in my attempt to get it perfect, I sometimes ruin it.

____ 4. Often, others think I do much more than what's requested of me.

____ 5. Now that I think about it, sometimes I keep doing a task as a way to escape.

Why would you engage in inappropriate hyper-focus? Perhaps because you can't move easily from one activity to another, you're escaping from stress, or you feel uncertain about what to do. For some people, the tendency toward perfectionism never lets them feel their job is finished. They spin their wheels and waste time.

You can probably spot inappropriate hyper-focus in others, but watch out! You might be blind about your own tendencies.

Assess: Keep a Hyper-Focus Diary

It's time to identify the activities that pull you in but also keep you stimulated long after it is appropriate or useful. Because you're so engaged in these activities, you're surprised when hours fly by and you discover you've left other duties undone. How often have you said, "Where did the time go?" You've drifted into a habit involving excessive and time-wasting behaviors. An example is spending half of one's free time watching television, something many Americans do.

Consider assessing your vulnerability to hyper-focus inappropriately. Use the following chart to collect information about what, where, when, and how long you engage in such activities. Write comments about your degree of productivity and your reactions when you hyper-focus.

Hyper-Focus Diary

What Activity Did I Do?	Date/Time/ Place?	How Long Did I Spend?	What was the Effect on Productivity and My Reactions?
Playing, practicing, or watching sporting events			
Watching television or movies			
Working on various hobbies			
Reading, playing, or listening to music			
Texting, twittering, or chatting (on a call or in person)			
Playing video, handheld, or computer games			
Surfing the Internet			
Other			

When you become more aware of the actual amount of time you spend on each activity, it's likely you'll decide that you waste more time than you'd like on certain activities.

Analyze the Consequences of Hyper-Focus

Assessing your situation helps you pinpoint both the negatives and positives of hyper-focus. On the plus side, while in hyper-focus mode, some people feel the flow—the steady, powerful mental energy that occurs when they focus intensely, sometimes for hours. When is hyper-focus inappropriate? If your performance reflects high highs, low lows, exhaustion, and poor results or you don't get other things done that need to be done, you might be engaging in inappropriate hyper-focus.

The overuse or abuse of one's ability to focus is the minus side. Either can occur when people spend excessive time doing such activities as shopping, gambling, or gaming. They get lost in time and space, squander money they can't afford to lose, and ignore their responsibilities. If at some point they have an awareness of being in overuse mode, perhaps they can avoid abuse and possible addiction. That's the time to seek help and stop the cycle.

Possible overuse or abuse is evident when others tell you to stop what you're doing. You reply, "Leave me alone. I need to do this now." You might be thinking, *I know I'm not doing the right thing, but I need to do this now. I can catch up on the other stuff tomorrow.* Of course, tomorrow never comes.

Use the following chart to analyze the consequences you experience if you engage in hyper-focus.

Balance of Consequences: Hyper-Focus

	Positive Consequences: Work / Home		Negative Consequences: Work / Home	
Short-term				
Long-term				

Set Realistic Goals and Monitoring Methods to Reduce Hyper-Focus Hassles

If you engage in activities that lead to inappropriate hyper-focus, then ask, "Does my behavior result in my being irresponsible, unproductive, or inconsiderate?" If your answer is yes (or maybe), then set a small goal based on reducing hyper-focus in one area while identifying an activity to replace it. For example, when Dwight is back at school, he registers for an online accounting course. To relax after dinner, he turns on the TV. But once he starts watching, he doesn't stop for hours. Sitting in front of the TV, he rushes through his accounting assignments. He doesn't take any breaks and falls asleep on the couch. Meanwhile, he's doing poorly on tests and courting a cycle of failure.

Here are Dwight's strategies to get out of hyper-focus mode and back on track.

- Put up this sign: TURN OFF THE TV. Set an alarm to remind me to turn off the television immediately after the evening news. Walk out of the room to my desk.

- Start on assignments. Work for about thirty minutes at a time, with five-minute breaks. Use a cell phone alarm to track the time.

- Monitor and motivate. Check off each small segment of work as I complete it. Then smile and say, "Good job. A little bit can go a long way."

When you feel stressed or fatigued, you're more susceptible to escapist activities (such as television or the Internet or working in "overkill" mode). Set a small, doable goal that will curb your inappropriate hyper-focus. You could monitor your progress by charting the days when you attempt to reduce the time spent on hyper-focus. Seek other ways to stay on track also. Too often, the *critical parent* in your head whispers that nothing is enough. Like a *good parent*, recognize your efforts when you've made progress.

If inappropriate hyper-focus seems like a potential barrier to your performance, use the following chart to help you plan your course of action.

Goals, Monitoring, and Motivation

Possible Goals	How Will I Monitor My Progress?	How Will I Motivate and Reinforce My Efforts?
1.		
2.		

Use Demon-Defying Strategies

After you collect information and form a plan, identify two or three activities that can stem your excessive hyper-focus habit. Remember the old adage, *"Actions speak louder than words."*

Consider the following strategies to avoid hyper-focus hassles.

___ *Use visualization.* "I can visualize how much better I worked last time when I set a timer to remind me to take a stretch break every thirty minutes."

___ *Use constructive self-talk.* Give yourself permission to work for shorter rather than longer periods, and include brief breaks. Say, "It isn't wasting time when I take breaks. If I don't take them, I end up spinning my wheels and getting lost on tangents."

___ *Use reason.* In the case of inappropriate focus, use your reasoning skills to remember the difference between short-term and long-term benefits. Perhaps choose a positive distraction that's pleasant and relaxing but doesn't drag you into overuse.

___ *Use positive assertiveness*: It's your right to set up positive conditions for productivity, especially when working in teams. Say, "I know some of you think that sitting for hours toughing it out as a team, military style, is productive, but it isn't for me. Aren't we at the point of diminishing returns? Why don't we take a break and take a fresh look in a few minutes?" Also, obtain clear instructions, goals, and timetables from supervisors so you know what to do and when. Otherwise, you could needlessly spin your wheels.

___ *Institute productive habits.* Set an alarm to break your work sessions into twenty- to forty-minute segments. Create a routine for meeting responsibilities rather than following your interests. For example, say, "I'll finish my paperwork and then work on my hobby. But first I'll turn on the timer so I don't work until dawn, like I did last week."

___ *Use the Stop, Look, and Listen technique*: Place this wording on a sticky note where you'll easily see it: STOP at the Five-Minute Warning to begin cleaning up at 10:30 p.m. As your eyes hit the note, you stop working, look around, and listen as you say, "Now's the time to straighten things out. That way I'll stop on time."

___ *Access social support.* Contact a friend and say, "Call me at nine in the evening to remind me to stop working and start cleaning up." You might mention the logic behind the request. For example, say, "When I work too long on the statistical analysis, I make careless mistakes. It's reasonable for me to spend about three hours today. I need to take breaks so I can remain accurate."

Greater awareness, coupled with strategy and action, will lessen your inappropriate hyper-focus, improve your productivity, and increase your satisfaction.

The Overstimulation of a Racing Mind

> *Carl has too much to do in too little time. He describes his feelings this way: "I just can't get my arms around all my thoughts and things I have to do." Summing up his situation, he says, "My mind is like a Lamborghini, but I have a Volkswagen transmission."*

Has your boss or friend ever said, "You're talking a mile a minute and jumping from topic to topic. Can't you slow down?" In response, you think, *What's wrong with that person? Do I have to spell out everything?* Better to ask, *Is a racing mind distracting me from getting my message across or doing the job well?*

To assess if your mind tends to race, read each item on the following list and check all that apply to you.

Self-Check: Racing Mind

_____ 1. People tell me to slow down and stick to the point when I'm explaining something.

_____ 2. My thoughts move too quickly, and I forget what I'm talking about.

_____ 3. I don't take time to finish one thing before I move to another.

_____ 4. I don't listen well. The phrase *in one ear and out the other* describes me well.

_____ 5. I speak too quickly when leaving messages on others' voice mails.

_____ 6. I'm overcommitted and flooded by thoughts of tasks that need doing.

If you check two or three items, you could benefit from consciously slowing down. This will increase your chances of completing more tasks, achieving greater accuracy, and communicating your message more effectively.

Why might your mind race? It's often due to a fast, impulsive thinking style and to overcommitment, overabundant creativity, or plain old stress. By nature, you might think and react quickly without adequate information, enough time to maintain a train of thought, or knowing all options. As a result, you don't provide what others need to understand the message you want to communicate.

Consider creativity to be a gift. But if it runs wild, you might fail to complete projects and feel unfulfilled. Here's an example of what can happen.

> *Harold, a gifted website designer, has developed his business to a profitable level. His creativity, however, is doing him in. He makes a plan for a new client but then is flooded with thoughts about how to improve an existing website. Before he knows it, he's ignored too many messages and feels exhausted. This leads to missed deadlines and overrun budgets. So he imposes a limit on the amount of creative time he devotes to a first draft. For example, he schedules two- to four-hour time slots to review the client's interests. Every half hour, he reminds himself, "This is a preliminary plan—only what's necessary for the client to see my creative approach and provide feedback. This is good planning and good customer service."*

Once Harold becomes aware of his vulnerability, he employs strategies to rein in his creativity and improve his productivity. He uses constructive self-talk to put time limits on his creativity-based projects so he can cover the boring ones. He uses a form of the Stop, Look, and Listen technique. For example, he works for a while and then stops, looks for better ways to work, and listens to the messages that motivate him.

Another factor contributing to having a racing mind is overcommitting your time and even your money. Learn to use your assertive skills to say no nicely yet firmly. This avoids being overwhelmed and saying, "I'll never get all of this done. I don't know where to start."

Without assertive responses, you can easily flit from thought to thought, unable to fully plan or solve problems. Circumstances like that can make you feel bad and stop working. Even with the ones you love, it's important to know how to say no in a nice way.

> *Cameron, an automotive executive, knows that his department is on the verge of closing. The timing couldn't be worse. His dad is post-surgery, his daughter is applying to colleges, and the values of his investments and pension plan are plummeting. Normally a competent person, Cameron's life circumstances are triggering a racing-mind effect. As a result, he finds it difficult to problem solve.*

Instead of living as if life is an emergency, Cameron needs quiet think time so he can better control his racing mind. In turn, this can help him problem solve and develop contingency plans.

Assess Your Racing Mind

When you see signs that your racing mind might derail your performance, collect more specific information about the when, where, and why of the difficulty. Use a rating scale from one to ten, with ten indicating the highest degree of interference posed by a racing mind at work, home, and other setting.

- Work 1   2   3   4   5   6   7   8   9   10
- Home 1   2   3   4   5   6   7   8   9   10
- Other 1   2   3   4   5   6   7   8   9   10

Also, you can draw on your experiences in this way.

- Describe situations in which you are most able to slow down and pay careful attention to a topic or task.

  _____

  _____

- Describe situations when you're least able or unable to avoid a racing mind.

  _____

  _____

- Describe triggers that appear to contribute to your racing mind, such as stress, over-commitment, unassertiveness, unbridled creativity, or ineffective listening.

  _____

  _____

- When you experience a racing mind, what's the effect on your:

- Attention: _____

- Memory: _____

- Organization: _____

- Stress (or energy) level: _____

- Productivity: _____

Analyze the Consequences of a Racing Mind

Consider the costs and benefits of your racing mind. On one hand, under pressure from financial and personal concerns, you might believe you can't rest for a moment. On the other hand, the more you allow your racing mind to drive your problem-solving and decision-making processes, the further behind you fall. A cycle ensues. Stress increases, insomnia occurs, and several demons join forces to exacerbate a downward spiral in your performance. As you attempt to complete tasks accurately, you miss details, make mistakes, or drift into tangents.

Sound familiar? If so, get those racing thoughts out of your head and onto paper. Engage in a brainstorming activity; list the major demands that keep you awake. You might need to access information sources or resources to do so.

Use the following worksheet for reviewing short-term and long-term consequences of a racing mind. Often, jotting down notes alone can clarify your thoughts and reduce stress. In addition, this worksheet provides a structured approach and a vehicle for discussing your concerns and options with others.

Balance of Consequences: Racing Mind

	Positive Consequences: Work / Home		Negative Consequences: Work / Home	
Short-term:				
Long-term:				

If you suffer exceptionally severe consequences from a racing mind over time, seek advice from an expert, such as a physician, psychologist, or other specialist. Realize that a racing mind can be a side effect of medication, a symptom of ADHD, or indication of emotional distress.

Set Realistic Goals and Monitoring Methods to Quell Your Racing Mind

To avoid the negative consequences associated with a racing mind, try setting a goal. Your goal can involve reducing the number of times your mind races in a day or the length of time it lasts.

Goals, Monitoring, and Motivation

Possible Goals	How Will I Monitor My Progress?	How Will I Get Motivated and Reinforce My Efforts?
1.		
2.		

Use Demon-Defying Strategies

A racing mind needs management. Schedule both short-term and long-term activities so you are dealing with one issue or task at a time. The following strategies can help you stop a racing mind and engage in effective problem solving—at least for a few minutes.

____ *Use visualization.* If your mind races, visualize yourself as a sprinter rather than a marathon runner. Your new approach is to work intensely for brief periods and then rest. When working in your area of greatest vulnerability, slow down and work for briefer periods than usual. Understanding your best pace for doing various types of tasks to avoid a racing mind is a key strategy that promotes effectiveness.

____ *Use reason.* Understand that a racing mind, by its nature, keeps generating ideas and projects. Say, "I need to write down these extra plans for later. Right now, I need to stay on track."

____ *Use constructive self-talk.* Spend a few minutes planning. Say, "I need to take five or ten minutes to plan. I'll do it now. The better my plan, the easier it will be to implement."

____ *Use positive assertiveness.* Stop the constant overwhelm and overcommitment that lead to jumping helter-skelter from one topic or task to another. Refuse to add to your already full plate and ask for help when you need it.

____ *Institute productive routines.* Conserve your energy, both physical and mental. Schedule work times for when you feel most alert, and plan to use your psychic energy in short, intense periods. Allow time and energy to slow down, focus, and schedule. Use a systematic approach. Break tasks into specific categories that you divide into small, doable segments and then do one thing at a time. For example, one author sets a timer to separate such tasks as brainstorming, organizing, writing, and editing.

___ *Use the Stop, Look, and Listen technique.* Stop as soon as you are aware that your mind is racing. Focus your mind's eye on the task at hand. Listen as you repeat a positive rule, such as "One step at a time."

___ *Access social support.* When your mind is racing, turn to someone to help you slow down and concentrate. Call a friend, a family member, or an expert in the field. Often, that trusted person can help talk you through a bothersome process or situation.

Disrupting Daydreaming, or Mind Wandering

"Dream when you're feeling blue. Dream, that's the thing to do." These words, written in 1944 by Johnny Mercer, attest to the fact that we all have the capacity use positive distractions when we feel sad or low. Daydreaming, therefore, can be helpful to divert attention from unpleasant thoughts or to inspire, provide rest, or reduce stress. Under these conditions, daydreaming, or mind wandering, sets the stage for creative thought or problem solving. If, however, you use daydreaming as an everyday escape from life's realities, then it can negatively affect your performance and productivity.

When your mind continually wanders to personal affairs while you're on the job, your productivity is diminished. If this happens to you, you're not alone. A 2009 survey indicated that a record number of people waste time at work; 64 percent of respondents reported wasting one hour or less each day. Some of the top time-wasting activities involved personal business, personal phone calls, and Internet use (*Journal of Accountancy*, 2009).

Use the following self-check to determine whether daydreaming, or mind wandering, is a serious distraction for you.

Self-Check: The Impact of Daydreaming

___ 1. I daydream more than I like.

___ 2. My mind wanders too frequently when I need to begin a task.

___ 3. My daydreaming negatively impacts my productivity during meetings.

___ 4. I feel overwhelmed and find that my mind wanders a lot.

___ 5. Others tell me I look as if my mind wanders.

If you checked more than two items, then daydreaming or a wandering mind affects your ability to pay attention at the level you need to meet your work/life responsibilities. Daydreaming may indicate that you need to take brief breaks when tasks are complex or boring.

Assess Daydreaming, or Mind Wandering

Keep track of the frequency, length, and effects of your daydreaming, or mind wandering, for a week. Once you've collected specific information about daydreaming, decide if it's interfering with your productivity.

Daydreaming Diary

Daydream	Date/ Time	Situation	What Happens?	What Was the Effect on My Work?	How Did I Feel?
1.					
2.					
3.					
4.					

Analyze the Consequences of Daydreaming, or Mind Wandering

When you inadvertently space out and look preoccupied, others might think you lack interest or respect. In some cases, your professional image is damaged; in other cases, your social or familial relationships suffer or your performance while playing sports or music falters. How often does another person say to you, "What are you thinking? Keep your mind on the game; you're messing up." For example, while your opponent serves the tennis ball, you're thinking of what to make for dinner, where you'll go after the game, or how to solve a problem at work.

Take time to think about the consequences of mind wandering, or daydreaming, in your work/life settings. The following chart will help.

Balance of Consequences: Daydreaming/Mind Wandering

	Positive Consequences: Work / Home		Negative Consequences: Work / Home	
Short-term:				
Long-term:				

Set Realistic Goals and Monitoring Methods to De-escalate Daydreaming

If you frequently daydream or let your mind wander and want to avoid the negative consequences that result, then set a goal. Your goal can involve reducing the number of times in a day you daydream or the length of time that it lasts.

Follow through by structuring tasks in ways that short-circuit daydreaming and channel creative impulses. What's your next step? To identify *doable* changes. On your calendar, schedule times and activities to ensure you can fully concentrate at particularly important times. Use a specific color marker to highlight times when you need your full attention. Is it during a dull but critical afternoon meeting?

You'll find that when you track your progress, it's easy to set a realistic goal and think about what actions will ensure that you attain the goal.

Goals, Monitoring, and Motivation

Possible Goals	How Will I Monitor My Progress?	How Will I Motivate and Reinforce My Efforts?
1.		
2.		

Issue and Strategies: Mind Wandering When Listening

It's important to ask, "How well do I listen to what others have to say?" Depending on your interest in the topic, you might only listen in spurts. You'll find it difficult to listen when your mind is busy with your own thoughts.

To improve your listening abilities, ask questions and restate others' messages to check for accuracy and discover underlying messages. For those with a racing mind, effective listening requires conscious effort. It's easy to lose the trust and rapport of those with whom you want to interact if you don't make the effort.

Issue and Strategies: Mind Wandering When Reading

Many workers today are returning to school to upgrade their skills or perhaps to change careers. But when they hit the books, their minds wander—especially if they've had a rough day at work. If you find your thoughts wandering when reading tedious or technical material or when you're tired, say, "I'll only do this task in short time segments" or "I'll begin with the first part and then review so I really understand it." While reading, keep refocusing your attention by asking, "What questions need to be answered?"

Daydreaming is nature's way of telling you to take a break. You may need to read intensely and then take a brief rest. The important point is not *how long* you read but *how well* you understand and remember the material. If you become fidgety, then stand and stretch or walk while reading. Keep active by using a white board to write and organize your notes. Alternatively, sit on a large athletic ball. It provides just enough "wiggle" to keep you alert while you're sitting.

Use Demon-Defying Strategies

Let's use the task of reading to illustrate how various strategies—active rather than passive—can be applied to prevent daydreaming.

___ *Use visualization.* Imagine the characters, plot, or main ideas after reading a title or book description. As you read, use your imagination to make a movie in your mind. Employ a similar process to summarize chapters or the book as a whole when you've finished reading it.

___ *Use reason.* Question the quality of your comprehension. Integrate thought into your reading or listening activities. Ask questions that require reflection and interpretation. For example, ask, "What are the underlying meanings? How does this section relate to other sections? How does this author compare to another?"

___ *Use constructive self-talk.* Describe the main ideas in your own words—an especially powerful technique when combined with visualization. Each process aids the other. Constructive self-talk can incorporate self direction. For example, how many times have you come to the end of a page, only to realize you have no idea what you've just read? Instead of saying, "How could I do that?" or "I'll never understand this," say, "Focus now. What's the question to address?"

___ *Use positive assertiveness.* Too often, readers are cowed by the myth that they must start at the beginning and read every word of every page. You are the boss of your reading. Decide what information you need from a particular source and read to find it. This type of seek-and-find strategy focuses your attention and relieves the time pressure caused by reading material that's not relevant to your needs.

___ *Institute productive habits.* Read for brief time segments and take frequent breaks to help you focus, concentrate, and retain information. The more often you read, the more efficient you become at finding information and enjoying the material. Set aside a period at least four times a week to read. They don't have to be long periods. Even twenty minutes can allow you to focus and gain information.

___ *Use the Stop, Look, and Listen technique.* Once you pose a question and read for the answer, you stop, look at a mental picture of what you read, and listen to a summary in your own words. This method helps you to incorporate a thinking process into your reading activity.

___ *Access social support.* Joining a book club or regularly discussing books with others can enhance the quality of the reading experience and deepen the sense of togetherness. Often, being part of a book club encourages you to read about topics you might otherwise miss.

John and Marsha's Unruly-Mind Success Story

How do two hassled, rushed, but creative professionals tend to the necessary but least inviting aspects of their jobs? It's common to put them off and then stress about the simple, tedious activities that need doing—especially when your mind races and you have a million things to do. To corral their very competent but somewhat unruly minds, John and Marsha team up regularly. Based on the idea of parallel play (in which young children play independently next to but not with each other), they designed a parallel work schedule. They meet early in the morning on Fridays for one or two hours. John has the coffee ready. The two of them spend a few minutes on "Hi—how are things going?" From that point on, they each attend to their own tasks independently. Their camaraderie fosters focus and energy, and their collaboration works like a charm!

In this situation, a collaborative situation imposes order and productivity on the creative but somewhat unruly mind. Knowing about protected time and having a supportive colleague creates conditions in which to get the odious tasks of one's job out of the way.

An unknown author said, "In the desert of life, the wise person travels by caravan, while the fool prefers to travel alone." With whom can you travel to better manage the Unruly-Mind Demon?

12

Maintenance, Meltdowns, and Peacefulness

Richie is an actuary, a person responsible for the analytical backbone of his company's financial situation. He needs to be alert, quiet, and able to concentrate to achieve the accuracy his job requires. Just when Richie thinks he's corralled the Demons of Distraction that once surrounded him at work, his department merges with another and moves to a temporary location. After enjoying a more stress-free working life, he's worried that all his hard work was in vain. Will he revert to his old habits— allowing others to interrupt him, not scheduling think and rest time, and maintaining his walks at lunchtime?

Richie should be concerned. Even when the conditions in which you work or play are stable, it's difficult to maintain the gains you achieve. For many, the trickiest aspect of any change effort is sticking to a plan. This occurs because, over time, you might lose interest or be distracted by other concerns. At some point, you realize your efforts have become inconsistent and your gains have dwindled. Your satisfaction suffers.

Over the long haul, how many of your friends or family become more successful when they get more exercise, eat healthier, stress less, sleep more, and keep a better eye on their finances? To make improvements as Richie did, you confront the Demons of Distraction, make resolutions, set goals, and start executing your plan. Before long, you realize that keeping your plan moving presents greater challenges than you anticipated. When you adopt the ideas in this chapter, however, you ensure long-term success.

Specifically, this chapter offers ways to monitor your workflow over time, maintain your progress, and enjoy a greater sense of peace. In addition, you'll find strategies for avoiding pitfalls and managing meltdowns, as well as charts to monitor productivity and lifestyle factors.

The Elusiveness of Maintenance

Maintenance is the most cumbersome part of the behavior-change process. Only between 8 percent and 12 percent of those who make New Year's resolutions keep them for more than a month or so (Shapiro, 2008). What does it take to make a plan and stick to it? It takes *a system, strategies,* and *support.*

The *system* advocated in this book is founded upon decades of research in behavioral-cognitive methodology. The five steps of the action plan or Plan of Attack are based on research that includes studies on self-regulation: assessing behavior, analyzing general and personal consequences, setting goals, and monitoring and reinforcing progress.

The *strategies,* also rooted in research, help to align your personal learning style and strengths with your unique needs. Most important, they help you to avoid predictable pitfalls.

The *support* comes from sharing your plans and progress with others and finding resources when progress slows down.

Yes, change—and maintaining that change—can be elusive because the behavior adjustments you seek seem so basic. It's astounding to think that, in many cases, the simpler a behavior seems, the more difficult it is to change. For example, you think, "It *shouldn't* be that hard to post a Do Not Disturb sign to hold the *Others* Demon at bay." Yet it is. You want to alter an ingrained habit, yet even after making initial improvements, you backslide. Inevitably you confront crisis-type situations that trigger negative emotional reactions—meltdowns—which in turn lead to interruptions in your productivity. How well do you stay on track, notice the red flags (possible pitfalls), and deal with unexpected difficulties? Use the following checklist to assess how well you are doing to stay on track.

Self-Check: Maintenance

Directions: Visualize events that occurred over the last weeks/months when you attempted to take actions against distractions. Then read the following statements and place a check next to all that apply to you.

　　　____ 1. I stay on track once I institute a plan of action.

　　　____ 2. I use such triggers as setting alarms to help me follow my plan of action.

　　　____ 3. I use charts or other ways of tracking progress to stay on track.

___ 4. I use supports like calendars and alarms to help me stay on track.

___ 5. I'm aware of possible, even predictable, pitfalls that can derail me.

___ 6. I effectively confront challenges and manage emotional responses so I can maintain consistency in my productivity.

Review and reflect about the statements you checked. Are you sticking to your plan? If not, what's wrong?

Major Strategy: Monitoring Work Flow

Constant vigilance is the key to continuous progress. Therefore, enhancing work/life productivity requires that you monitor your attention, organization, memory, and workflow processes. If you don't have a systematic way of monitoring how much and how well your work flows through the day and week, you create a situation that leaves you particularly vulnerable to distractions. In such cases, the Demons of Distraction can be unrelenting.

Knowing about these demons gives you the power to build your defenses. Awareness, however, takes you only so far. Select the strategies that will reduce the distractions and increase your chances for greater productivity, and then *take action*. This requires being mindful of your flow of mental energy and problem-solving capacity day and night.

Monitoring your behaviors and feelings is aided by a checklist, chart, and/or schedule. Review what worked and what didn't work and keep adjusting to fix what doesn't work. For example, you could:

- Post the a checklist near your work area

- Use a kitchen or other timer to check your work every fifteen to thirty minutes

- Ask, "What feelings tend to reduce my motivation or productivity? Do I need a break, better instructions, or more support?"

As you become more aware of your feelings and their effects, you can modulate them so you realize new levels of productivity. If you don't experience the progress you desire, use a technique like Stop, Look, and Listen. Stop to reflect and review, asking, "What's holding me back?" Look at the situation and your actions (or non-actions). Listen as you describe times when you attained success and the actions you took. From there, use your logic and knowledge of productive strategies to adjust your plan and your behavior.

Issue and Strategies: Life Style and Productivity

Enhancing work productivity often hinges on aspects of your lifestyle. Whenever productivity and workflow seem to be problematic, you will benefit from reexamining lifestyle factors. For example, when you are fatigued during the day, you increase your vulnerability to mistakes and irritability. You have little patience to implement routines that you know are beneficial. In addition, when you're overly fatigued, your resistance to illness may be lowered; when you have colds, etc., it's difficult to work. Therefore, you need to disallow distraction from interfering with your efforts to stay healthy. Don't let the demons gang up and bring you down. Engage in regular exercise, eat nutritious meals, get adequate rest, use social support, and manage your stress. These factors also affect your time management and productivity. You might find that one factor can trigger a domino effect—that is, you stay up too late working on a project and experience grumpiness and inactivity the next day. To boot, you're so tired that you don't exercise. It's easy to slip if you deny or lack full awareness of the effects of each of these factors on your productivity, health, and sense of well-being.

Here's a chart to keep track of how you're doing. On the same day each week, rank the level of success for each factor on a scale from one to ten, with ten representing the highest.

Managing Life Style and Productivity

	Lowest 1	2	3	4	5	6	7	8	9	Highest 10
Good Sleep Hygiene										
Proper Nutrition										
Regular Exercise										
Effective Stress Management										
Competent Illness/ Medication Management										
Productive Work/Life										

Review the results by answering such questions as these:

- Which items do I rate the highest and lowest? _____

  _____

- How focused and productive am I? _____

- How does fatigue relate to memory or organization? _____

- How are my health-related behaviors linked to my productivity? _____

- Am I taking medications as prescribed? Do they have side effects that affect my thinking or mood? _____

- What are the patterns or trends? _____

- Am I trying to do too much at one time? _____

- Are there lessons to learn, given my self-rating? _____

- What doable goals are next for me? _____

Act as your own coach by asking and answering questions as you review your progress. Identify the factors that help or hinder your productivity and performance. The information you gain will help you identify what to maintain and what to modify.

Issue and Strategies: Incentives, Feedback, and Rewards

Many people assume they should be able to do everything that's necessary—all the time. In some instances, you can accomplish many of those *shoulds*, especially in areas of your strength and interest.

Unfortunately, not every task you must do is interesting or falls in your area of greatest strength. In addition, life's distractions can get in the way of your best intentions, even when you work under ideal conditions. For long-term productivity, even very bright, competent, and motivated people need to consciously monitor performance and productivity so they can maintain positive results.

Setting the right stage for productive behavior and providing rewards to recognize your achievements are essential. Checklists and charts help you track your progress and identify information about adjustments to make; you'll also learn when some type of reward or reinforcement keeps the action going. Even the smallest recognition helps. For example, for a long-term project, you might:

- Use a chart to check off daily progress and feel proud that you've accomplished something each day.

- Enjoy a small reward once a week after you've completed what you wanted.

- Plan a special reward like a getaway weekend if you maintain the routine for several months.

- Visualize your steady progress toward your goal, smile, and give yourself a mental pat on the back.

- Congratulate yourself often, saying, "I felt uncomfortable limiting the Open Door Policy, but at least I have some time to think!"

- Share your progress with those who care; bask in the glow of their praise.

Without feedback, incentives, and rewards, it's easy to regress, especially when you need to do unpleasant, difficult, or boring tasks.

Charlie's Productivity Success Story

> *I watch my dad Charlie resting on the couch; eyes closed, his hands folded on the newspaper that lies upon his chest. He's mumbling. I think, This is weird. I say, "Daddy, what are you doing?" Patiently, he replies, "After every day in the store, I imagine each customer who came in. I think about what happened and how I could have done a better job. Then I know what to try the next day."*

You met Charlie Ponte earlier. He's my dad, who taught me a lot about actions against distractions. His strategies evolved as he survived and thrived as a merchant. As I reviewed his behavior, it seemed that he used a variety of activities that are described in the research, including visualizing, assessing, employing constructive self-talk, and goal setting. Always focused on his customers, Charlie's attitude served him well—except for the time he was so hyper-focused that he failed to sign his lease and suffered a major financial loss.

> *Charlie emigrated from Sicily as a four-year-old child and had no formal education after the sixth grade. Yet he started a musical instrument*

business in midtown Manhattan with only one saxophone. He ended up with a thriving business in a building he owned and lived in. As so many entrepreneurs of his era, Charlie built his business by trial and error. To survive, he refused to be distracted from his overall vision. Each day, he took time to use his logic and review his performance with customers. He developed a plan and implemented strategies. He didn't take success for granted. Expecting the road to be rough, he monitored and adjusted his behavior as needed.

Today, we live in times of unexpected turbulence, and distractions plague young and old alike. Whether stories about immigrants of yesteryear or the knowledge of contemporary researchers inspire us, we thrive on a sense of optimism coupled with a passion for action.

Taking action fights the constant distraction, disorganization, and forgetfulness that might undermine your performance today. With action comes an increased sense of self-control and self-satisfaction. In essence, action enables you to make such statements as "I'm making progress" or "I know how to adjust" or "I tried my best."

So identify the activities that fritter away your time and energy. Create a Plan of Attack for each day. When you're most alert, work on tasks that require your thinking skills or creative talents. Most important, make a public commitment to reduce needless distractions.

When you take actions against distractions, you banish the Demons of Distraction from your work/life and enjoy better memory and organization. You'll also feel more productive than ever—and infinitely more satisfied with your work/life.

References and Resources

AAA Foundation. "Distracted Driving the Top Reason that 35 Percent of Drivers Feel Less Safe Than Five Years Ago." http://www.aaafoundation.org/multmedia/indes.cfm?button=2000TSCIndex.

American Institute of Stress. "Job Stress." http://www.stress.org/job.htm.

Alberti, R., and M. Emmons. *Your Perfect Right: Assertiveness and Equality in Your Life and Relationships.* 9th ed. San Obispo, CA: Impact Publishers, 2008.

Allen, D. *Getting Things Done: The Art of Stress-Free Productivity.* New York: Penguin Group, 2001.

Alpert, J. D. "Failing Grades in the Adoption of Healthy Lifestyle Choices." *The American Journal of Medicine* (May 29, 2009).

American Psychological Association. "Stress in America." 2010. http://www.apa.org/news/press/releases/stress/national-report.pdf.

Anderson, N. B. "Understanding Stress in America." *Monitor on Psychology* (January 2011): 9. http://www.stressinamerica.org.

Associated Press. "Science paying attention to not paying attention. Why is the mind wired to wander every chance it gets?" http://www.msnbc.msn.com/id/17690541/ns/health-mental_health/.

Barkley, R. A., with C. Benton. *ADHD and the Nature of Self-Control.* New York: Guilford Press, 2005.

_____. *Taking Charge of Adult ADHD.* New York: Guilford Press, 2010.

Beck, J. S. *Cognitive Therapy: Basics and Beyond.* New York: Guilford Press, 1995.

Bishop, S. *Develop Your Assertiveness.* London: Kogan Page, 2006.

Blumenthal, J. M., M. Babyak, J. Wei, C. O'Connor, R. Waugh, E. Eisenstein, D. Mark, A. Sherwood, P. S. Woodley, R. J. Irwin, and G. Reed. "Usefulness of psychosocial treatment of mental stress-induced myocardial ischemia in men." *American Journal of Cardiology* 89 (2002): 164–68.

Boekaerts, M., P. R. Pintrich, and M. Zeidner (eds.). *Academic Handbook for Self-Regulation*. San Diego: Academic Press, 2005.

Bower, S. A., and G. H. Bower. *Asserting Yourself: A Practical Guide for Positive Change*. Cambridge, MA: Da Capo Press, 2004.

Brown, T. E. *ADHD Comorbidities: Handbook for ADHD Complications in Children and Adults*. Washington, DC: American Psychiatric Press, 2009.

_____. *Attention Deficit Disorder: The Unfocused Mind in Children and Adults*. New Haven, CT: Yale University Press, 2005.

_____. "Executive Functions: Describing Six Aspects of a Complex Syndrome." *Attention Magazine* (February 2008): 12–17.

Brownlow, M. "8 e-mail statistics to use at parties." 2009. http://www.e-mail-marketing-reports.com/iland/2009/08/8-e-mail-statistics-to-use-at-parties.html.

Bureau of Labor Statistics. American Time Use Survey—2009 Results. Washington, DC: US Department of Labor, June 22, 2010.

Cave, D. "Legal Drugs Kill Far More Than Illegal, Florida Says." *New York Times*. July 14, 2008. A10.

Carlin, G. "Stuff." http://www.bing.com/videos/watch/video/george-carlin-talks-about-stuff/48faad387fac0385387948faad387fac03853879700996715564?q=George+Carlin+on+StuffandFORM=VIRE2.

Carsia, T. "Design Workspaces for Higher Productivity." *Occupational Health and Safety* 71, no. 9 (September 2002).

Centazzo, T. "Employers: Address Job-Related Stress in Your Workplace for Healthier Employees and Bigger Profits." 2008. http://www.mblwellness.com/community/job-related-stress.htm.

Centers for Disease Control and Prevention. "Leading Causes of Death." 2007. http://www.cdc.gov/nchs/fastats/lcod.htm.

____. "Obesity." 2007–2008. http://www.cdc.gov/nchs/fastats/overwt.htm.

Charles, C. L., and M. Donaldson. *Bless Your Stress*. East Lansing, MI: Yes! Press, 2006.

Chen, B. *Always On: How the iPhone Unlocked the Anything, Anytime, Anywhere Future—and Locked Us In*. Philadelphia: Da Capo Press, 2011.

CNN. "Dangers of energy drinks." http://thechart.blogs.cnn.com/2011/02/14/pediatricians-parents-warned-on-energy-drink-dangers/.

Croasdale, M. "Fatal errors more likely on 24-hour call: Harvard sleep scientists say residents' hours still put patients at risk." 2007. http://www.amaassn.org/amednews/2007/01/22/prsb0122.htm.

Cutrell, E., M. Czerwinski, and E. Horvitz. "Notification, Disruption, and Memory: Effects of Messaging Interruptions on Memory." Interact Conference Proceedings. Tokyo, Japan: 2001.

Czeisler, C. "Harvard Medical School." *Public Library of Science (PloS) Medicine*. 2006.

____. "It's time to reform work hours for resident physicians." *Science News* 176, no. 9 (Oct. 24, 2009): 36. http://www.sciencenews.org/view/generic/id/48153/title/Comment_It%E2%80%99s_time_to_reform_work_hours_for_resident_physicians.

Davis, R. "Jonathan Franzen's 'book of the century' pulped over error." *Guardian*. http://www.guardian.co.uk/books/2010/oct/01/jonathan-franzen-book-pulped.

Daily Mail. "Pulped Fiction: Jonathan Franzen's latest novel recalled because it's full of mistakes."

http://www.dailymail.co.uk/news/article-1317086/Jonathan-Franzens-novel-Freedom-recalled-contains-mistakes.html.

____. "Three deaths linked to energy drink." http://www.dailymail.co.uk/health/article-59862/Three-deaths-linked-energy-drink.html.

Dell, M., with C. Fredman. *Direct from Dell: Strategies that Revolutionized an Industry.* New York: HarperCollins Publishers, 1999.

Depression Guideline Panel. "Depression in Primary Care: Volume 2." *Treatment of Major Depression. Clinical Practice Guideline,* no. 5 (1993): US Dept. HHS, AHCPR Publication 93-0551.

(The) Editors. "Workplace interruptions cost US economy $588bn a year." *Financial Express.* Besex, Inc. January 9, 2006. http://www.basex.com/press.nsf/0/E53F4C614 2D119A6852570F9001AB0EC?OpenDocument.

Ellis, A. *Feeling Better, Getting Better, Staying Better: Profound Self-Help Therapy for Your Emotions.* Atascadero, CA: Impact Publishers, 2001.

Ellis, A., and R. S. Harper. *A New Guide to Rational Living.* Chatsworth, CA: Wilshire Book Company, 1997.

Fackler, M. "International Business; President of Tokyo Stock Exchange Resigns." *New York Times.* December 21, 2005. Business Section, p. 1. http://query.nytimes.com/ gst/fullpage.html?res=9F0CEED61730F932A15751C1A9639C8B63&scp=2&sq=Pres ident%20of%20Tokyo%20Stock%20Exchange%20Resigns%202005&st=Search.

Feigelson, S. *Energize Your Meetings with Laughter.* Alexandria, VA: Association for Supervision and Curriculum Development, 1998.

Feiler, B. "Should You Google at Dinner?" *New York Times.* Sunday, December 12, 2010. Business Section, p. 2.

Finkelstein, K. E. "In Concert, Searchers Retrieve Yo-Yo Ma's Lost Stradivarius." *New York Times.* October 17, 1999. http://www.nytimes.com/1999/10/17/nyregion/in-concert-searchers-retrieve-yo-yo-ma-s-lost-stradivarius.html?page.

Forsyth, J., and F. Eifert. *Mindfulness and Acceptance Workbook for Anxiety.* Oakland, CA: New Harbinger, Inc., 2007.

Fuller, R. "Driver gets jail in nail-polish crash." *Chicago Tribune.* July 23, 2010. Section 1, p. 11.

Gardner, J. *7 Intelligences.* New York: Basic Books, 2006.

Gatyas, F. "IMS Institute Reports U.D. Spending on Medicines Grew 2.3 Percent in 2010, to 307.4 Billion." *IMS Institute for Healthcare Informatics*. http://www.google. com/search?sourceid=navclient&ie=UTF-8&rlz=1T4ADFA_enUS383US383&q=IM S+Health+dollars+spent+on+prescription+drugs.

Gill, A. "Now Don't Hear This." *New York Times*. May 2, 2010. Sunday Opinion, p. 11.

Gillies, R. "Coffee spill causes diversion for US flight." http://news.yahoo.com/s/ ap/20110105/ap_on_fe_st/cn_canada_plane_diverted.

Gittleman, L. "Texting or cell phone use may have caused fatal crash." *Morning Sun*. May 4, 2011. http://www.themorningsun.com/articles/2011/05/04/news/ doc4dc06aa58587b961463279.txt.

Gold, A. J. "What Fitness has done for me." http://www.healthchecksystems.com/ success.htm.

Greenbaum, J., and G. Markel. *Finding Your Focus: Practical Strategies for the Everyday Challenges Facing Adults with ADD*. New York: McGraw-Hill, 2005.

Greenberger, D., and C. Padesky. *Mind over Mood: Change How You Feel by Changing the Way You Think*. New York: Guilford Press, 1995.

Groeninger, A., and L. Black. "Metra Expands Quiet Cars to All Lines." *Chicago Tribune*. June 6, 2001. http://articles.chicagotribune.com/2011-06-06/news/ct-met-quiet-cars-20110606_1_quiet-cars-metra-s-electric-rock-island-line.

Grynbaum, M. M. "Her Work Goes Missing in a Cab, And Roberta Flack Can't Let it Be." *New York Times*. April 12, 2010. http://cityroom.blogs.nytimes.com/2010/04/12/ roberta-flack-meets-a-big-yellow-taxi/#more-157723.

Gu, Q., C. G. Dillon, and V. L. Burt. "Prescription Drug Use Continues to Increase: U.D. Prescription Drug Data for 2007–2008." Centers for Disease Control and Prevention NCHS Data Brief, Number 42. September 2010. http://www.cdc.gov/ nchs/data/databriefs/db42.htm.

Hallowell, E. M. *CrazyBusy: Overstretched, Overbooked, and About To Snap!* New York: Ballentine Books, 2006.

____. "My Wonderful ADHD 'Turbo' Brain." *Attitude Magazine*. December/January 2008. http://www.additudemag.com/adhd/article/2996.html.

Hallowell, E. M., and J. J. Ratey. *Delivered from Distraction: Getting the Most Out of Life with Attention Deficit Disorder.* New York: Ballantine Books, 2005.

____. *Driven to Distraction: Recognizing and Coping with Attention Deficit Disorder from Childhood through Adulthood.* New York: Pantheon Books, 1995.

Hanes, S. "Risky Business: Driving While Distracted." *Christian Science Monitor.* November 1, 2009. pp. 13–16.

Hayes, K. *Move Your Body: Tone Your Mood.* Oakland, CA: New Harbinger Publications, 2002.

Hayes, S. C., V. M. Follette, and M. M. Linehan. *Mindfulness and Acceptance: Expanding the Cognitive-Behavioral Tradition.* New York: Guilford Press, 2004.

Hayes, S. C., with S. Smith. *Get Out of Your Mind and Into Your Life: The New Acceptance and Commitment Therapy.* Oakland, CA: News Harbinger Publications, 2005.

Heydlauff, P. "Reducing Office Clutter." *EHS Today: The Magazine for Environment, Health and Safety Leaders.* March 1, 2009. http://ehstoday.com/safety/management/reducing-office-clutter-0309/.

Heylighen, F., and V. Clement. "Getting Things Done: The Science behind Stress-Free Productivity." ECCO-Evolution, Complexity and Cognition Research Group. Free University of Brussels, Brussels, Belgium. http://pespmc1.vub.ac.be/papers/GTD-cognition.pdf.

Hickey, A. R. "Smartphones, PDAs Left in Cabs at Alarming Rates." December 13, 2006. SearchMobileComputing.com. http://www.computerweekly.com/news/1280096088/Smartphones-PDAs-left-in-cabs-at-alarming-rates.

Hoyert, D. L., and J. Xu. "Deaths: Preliminary Data for 2011." Centers for Disease Control and Prevention. National Vital Statistics Report 61, no. 6 (October 10, 2012).

"The Internet Big Picture: World Internet Users and Population Statistics." Miniwatts Marketing Group. 2010. http://www.internetworldstats.com/stats.htm.

Jacobs, C., and I. Wendel. *Guide to Adult ADD/ADHD.* Avon, MA: Adams Media, 2010.

Jacobs, G. D., E. F. Pace-Schott, R. Stickgold, and M. W. Otto. "Cognitive Behavior Therapy and Pharmacotherapy for Insomnia." *Archives of Internal Medicine* 164 (2004): 1888–96. http://archinte.ama-assn.org/cgi/content/abstract/164/17/1888.

Jenkins, S. B. "Concerning Interruptions." *IEEE Computer* 39, no. 11 (November 2006).

Johnsgard, K. *Conquering Depression and Anxiety through Exercise*. Amherst, NY: Prometheus Books, 2004.

Journal of Accountancy: "Record Number of People Waste Time at Work." February 2009. http://www.journalofaccountancy.com/Issues/2009/Feb/WasteTimeatWork.htm.

Kabat-Zinn, J., A. O. Massion, J. Kristeller, L. G. Peterson, K. Fletcher, L. Pbert, W. Linderking, and S. F. Santorelli. "Effectiveness of a meditation-based stress reduction program in the treatment of anxiety disorders." *American Journal of Psychiatry* 149 (1992):936–43.

Kanfer, F., and A. P. Goldstein. *Helping People Change*. 2nd ed. New York: Pergamon Press, Inc., 1980.

Kavanagh, J. "Airline Pilots Struggle to Stay Focused." http://www.cnn.com/2009/TRAVEL/10/28/pilots.cockpit/index.html.

Klingberg, T. *The Overflowing Brain*. Oxford, England: Oxford University Press, 2009.

Kolberg, J. *Conquering Chronic Disorganization*. Decatur, IL: Squall Press, 1999.

Kolberg, J., and K. Nadeau. *ADD-Friendly Ways to Organize Your Life*. New York: Burnner-Routledge, 2002.

Kulawitz, H. J. "Pro Bono Piano." As told to Eilene Zimmerman. *Fortune Small Business*. February 18, 2008. http://money.cnn.com/2008/02/18/smbusiness/pro_bono_biano.fsb/index.htm.

Lazonick, W., and O. Tulum. Sloan Industry Report. 2010. http://isapapers.pitt.edu/161/1/wp-2010-01-lazonick.pdf.

Lyall, S. "Is this the Gaffe that Breaks a Premier's Back?" *New York Times*. April 29, 2010. International Section, pp. A1, A6.

Lyubomirsky, S., L. A. King, and E. Diener. "The benefits of frequent positive affect: Does happiness lead to success?" *Psychological Bulletin* 131 (2005): 803–55.

Madvin, G., and G. Markel. *Finding Happiness during Turbulent Times: Using Aristotle's Ideas as an Action Guide.* Bloomington, IN: iUniverse, 2012.

Markel, G. *Defeating the 8 Demons of Distraction: Proven Strategies to Increase Productivity and Decrease Stress.* Lincoln, NE: iUniverse, 2008.

_____. "Distractibility, Inattention, and Disorganization: Do I have ADD or ADHD?" *Selfgrowth.com.* June 21, 2009. http://www.selfgrowth.com/print598043.

McCarthy, T., and L. Fisher. "Heidi Montag Plastic Surgeon Frank Ryan Texting before Fatal Crash." Aug. 18, 2010. http://abcnews.go.com/Entertainment/heidi-montag-plastic-surgeon-frank-ryan-texting-car/story?id=11427497.

McKinley, Y., J., and M. L. Wald. "California Bans Texting by Operators of Trains." *New York Times.* September 19, 2008. p. 110.

McKnight-Eily, L. R., Y. Liu, G. S. Perry, L. R. Presley-Cantrell, T. W. Strine, H. Lu, and J. B. Croft. "Perceived Insufficient Rest or Sleep Among Adults." Division of Adult and Community Health, National Center for Chronic Disease Prevention and Health Promotion, Center for Disease Control. The Morbidity and Mortality Weekly Report 58, no. 42 (October 30, 2008): 1175–79. http://www.cdc.gov/mmwr/preview/mmwrhtml/mm5842a2htm.Microsoft. "To-do lists." http://www.microsoft.com/presspass/press/2008/jan08/0114NGOMPR.mspx.

Microsoft.. "Meetings. Two Wasted Days at Work: CNN/Money. New York. http://money.cnn.com/2005/03/16/technology/survey/index.htm.

_____. "To-do Lists. http://www.microsoft.com/presspass/press/2009/jan08/0114NGOMPR.mspx

Miller, J., K. Fletcher, and J. Kabat-Zinn. "Three-year follow-up and clinical implications of a mindfulness-based stress reduction intervention in the treatment of anxiety disorders." *General Hospital Psychiatry* 17 (1995):192–200.

Modern Museum of Art. *HELP! A Record Book for Household Names, Notes, and Numbers.* Boston: Little, Brown and Company, 1996.

National Highway Transportation Safety Administration (NHTSA). "Drowsy driving." http://www.nhtsa.gov/people/injury/drowsy_driving1/drowsyref.html.

National Institute of Mental Health. "The Numbers Count: Mental Disorders in America." Booklet.US Department of Health and Human Services. National Institutes of Health. 2006.

_____. "When Worry Gets Out of Control: Generalized Anxiety Disorder." Booklet. US Department of Health and Human Services. National Institutes of Health. 2007.

National Institute on Drug Abuse. http://www.emprc.org/resources/fact-sheets/nida-research-report-prescription-drug-abuse-and-addiction.

National Sleep Foundation. "Drowsy Driving.org. Facts and Stats." August 11, 2011. http://drowsydriving.org/about/facts-and-stats/.

National Sleep Foundation Survey. "Too Late Watching TV." http://www.sleepfoundation.org/article/how-much-sleep-do-we-really-need.

News, Bureau of Labor Statistics. "Number of Jobs Held, Labor Market Activities, and Earning Growth Among the Youngest Baby Boomers-Results from a Longitudinal Study." United States Department of Labor. June 27, 2008. http://www.bls.gove/nls.

Nielsen Online. "Global Faces and Networked Places: A Nielsen Report on Social Networking's New Global Footprint." March 2009. http://www.nielsen.com/us/en/insights/reports-downloads/2009/Social-Networking-New-Global-Footprint.html.

Novotney, A. "Get Your Clients Moving: Ten tips to incorporate exercise into your treatment arsenal." *Monitor on Psychology*. July/August 2008. pp. 68–69.

_____. "Silence, Please: Psychologists are increasing awareness of the harmful effects noise has on cognition and health." *Monitor on Psychology*. July/August 2011. pp. 46–49.

Orlowski, A. "The Shocking Truth about DAD." *Esquire*. January 2011. pp. 125–33.

Petz, J. *Boring Meetings Suck: Get More Out of Meetings, or Get Out of More Meetings.* New York, NY: Wiley and Sons, 2011.

Pogue, D. "Your Phone Is Locked. Just Drive." *New York Times.* April 29, 2010. Business Section, pp. B1, B9.

Posen, D. T. *The Little Book of STRESS RELIEF.* Buffalo, NY: A Firefly Book, 2004.

Price, M. "The Risks of Night Work." *Monitor on Psychology.* January 2011. pp. 39–41.

Radicati Group, Inc. "Guidelines for Managing Your Work and Personal E-mail."April 28, 2011. http://www.radicati.com/?page_id=46.

Ramsay, J. R., and A. L. Rostain. *Cognitive-Behavior Therapy for Adult ADHD.* New York: Routledge, 2008.

Rand, G. A. "Superorganized Traveler Who Once Forgot Something." *New York Times.* March 16, 2010. p. B6.

Ratey, J. J. *SPARK: The Revolutionary New Science of Exercise and the Brain.* New York: Little, Brown and Company, 2008.

____. *A User's Guide to the Brain: Perception, Attention, and the Four Theaters of the Brain.* New York: Vintage Books, 2001.

Ratey, J. J., and C. Johnson. *Shadow Syndromes: The Mild Forms of Major Mental Disorders That Sabotage Us.* New York: Bantam Books, 1998.

The Real Time Report. "Social Networks." http://therealtimereport.com/2010/03/22/94smillion-social-network-users-worldwide/.

Rosekind, M. R., K. B. Gregory, M. Mallis, S. L. Brandt, B. Seal, and D. Lerner. "The Cost of Poor Sleep: Workplace Productivity Loss and Associated Costs." *Journal of Occupational and Environmental Medicine* 52, no. 1 (January 2010): pp. 91–98.

Rothwell, W. J., C. K. Hohne, and S. B. King. *Human Performance Improvement.* 2nd ed. New York: Elsevier, 2007.

Rubin, R. "FDA Dispenses Opioid Concern." *USA Today.* February 10, 2009. p. 7D.

Rummler, F. S., and A. P. Brache. *Improving Performance.* 2nd ed. San Francisco: Jossey-Bass Publishers, 1995.

Saad, L. "On-the-Job Stress is US Workers' Biggest Complaint." http://www.gallup.com/poll/142715/job-stress-workers-biggest-complaint.aspx.

Salemi, V. "Best Sleep Products." http://www.aolhealth.com/health/sleep-well-sleep-better/feature/_a/best-sleep-products/2008.

Sarris, S. M. *Adult ADD: A Guide for the Newly Diagnosed.* Oakland, CA: New Harbinger Publications, Inc., 2011.

Schulz, R., and P. R. Sherwood. "Physical and Mental Health Effects of Family Caregiving." *Journal of Social Work Education* 44, no. 3 (2008 Fall Supplement): pp. 105–13.

Schwartz, N. D., and L. Story. "When Machines Take Control: High-Speed Glitch in Trading Costs Investors Millions." *New York Times.* Business Day Section, pp. B1, B7.

Seligman, M. E. P. *Authentic Happiness: Using the New Positive Psychology to Realize Your Potential for Lasting Fulfillment.* New York: Free Press, 2002.

_____. *Flourish: A Visionary New Understanding of Happiness and Well-Being.* New York: Free Press, 2011.

_____. *Learned Optimism.* New York: Knopf, 1991.

Shapiro, Stephen. 2008. http://www.steveshapiro.com/2008/12/11/interesting-new-years-resolution-statistics/.

Shontell, A. "Workers' Lack of Sleep Costs Employers Millions Each Year." January 13, 2011. http://www.buinessinsider.com/workers-lack-of-sleep-costs-employer-millions-of-dollars-each-year.

Silver, L. B. *Attention-Deficit Hyperactivity Disorder.* 2nd ed. Washington, DC: American Psychiatric Publishing, Inc., 1992.

Sloan Survey. "Class Differences: Online Education in the United States." Eighth Annual Sloan Survey of Online Education. 2010. http://sloanconsortium.org/publications/survey/survey.

Smith, C. "Twitter User Statistics Show Stunning Growth." *The Huffington Post.* March 14, 2011. http://www.huffingtonpost.com/2011/03/14/twitter-user-statistics_n_835581.html.

Solden, S. *Journeys Through ADDulthood: Discover a New Sense of Identity and Meaning with Attention Deficit Disorder.* New York: Walker Publishing Company, Inc., 2002.

____. *Women with Attention Deficit Disorder: Embrace Your Differences and Transform Your Life.* Nevada City, CA: Underwood Books, 2003.

Spira, J., and J. B. Feintuch. "The Cost of Not Paying Attention: How Interruptions Impact Knowledge Worker Productivity: Executive Summary." Basex, Inc. 2005. http://www.basex.com.

Spiro, J. B. "Information Overload Now $997 Billion: What Has Changed?" Basex Corporation. 2010. http://www.basexblog.com /2010/12/16/io997.

Stanford News. "Multitasking." http://news.standford.edu/pr/2009/ multitask-research-release-082409.html.

Steele, P. "We're Sorry This Is Late … We Really Meant to Post It Sooner: Research into Procrastination Shows Surprising Findings." *Science Daily.* University of Calgary. January 10, 2007. Retrieved January 10, 2011, from http://www.sciencedaily.com / releases/2007/01/070110090851.htm.

Stelzner, M. A. "2011 Social Media Marketing Industry Report." http://www. socialmediaexaminer.com/SocialMediaMarketingReport2011.pdf.

Stobbe, M. "CDC: Sleep Deprivation Affects a Third of Americans." *Huffington Post.* March 3, 2011. http://www.huffingtonpost.com/2011/03/03/cdc-sleep_n_831005. html.

Strosahl, K., and P. Robinson. *The Mindfulness and Acceptance Workbook for Depression.* Oakland, CA: New Harbinger, Inc., 2008.

Sylvestre-Williams, R. "How Recruiters Use LinkedIn." http://www.forbes.com/sites/ reneesylvestrewilliams/2012/05/31/how-recruiters-use-linkedin/.

Taylor, S. E., L. B. Pham, I. D. Rivkin, and D. A. Armor. "Harnessing the Imagination: Mental Simulation, Self-Regulation, and Coping." *American Psychologist* 53, no. 4 (April 1998): 429–39.

Tucker, M. "Daytime Nap Can Benefit a Person's Memory Performance." *Science Daily*. February 3, 2008. http://www.sciencedaily.com/releases/2008.

Tuckman, A. *More Attention, Less Deficit: Success Strategies for Adults with ADD*. Plantation, FL: Specialty Press, 2009.

UK Search Engine Marketing Agency. "2011 Social Media Statistics Show Huge Growth." http://www.browsermedia.co.uk/2011/03/30/2011-social-media-statistics-show-huge-growth.

University of Chicago. "Sleep Helps People Learn Complicated Tasks." *Science Daily*. Retrieved November 23, 2008 from http://www.sciencedaily.com/releases/2008/11/081117110838.htm.

Vaux, A. *Social Support: Theory, Research, and Intervention*. New York: Praeger Publishers, 1988.

Wachter, D., and L. Stark. "Tired? Study Says Americans Need More Sleep." February 8, 2008. http://abcneews.go.com/CleanPrint/cleanprintproxy.aspx?1295304791834.

Wang, S. S. "When Mixing Medications Can Be Deadly." *Wall Street Journal*. February 7, 2008. p. D1.

Watson, D. L., and R. Tharp. *Self-Directed Behavior: Self-Modification for Personal Adjustment*. Belmont, CA: Wadsworth Publishing, 2002.

Wechsler, H. "Distractions Disrupt Your Brain." 2009. http://knol.google.com/k/hal-wechsler/distractions-distrupt-your-brain/2ev4j1ajanehw2/6.

Weir, K. "Scents and Sensibility." http://www.infoplease.com/ipa/A0005110.html (February 2011): pp. 41–44.

Welsh, T. "Seeing vs Believing." *Journal of Human Movement Science*. University of Calgary. December 2007. http://scholar.google.com/scholar?q=T.+Welsh+Journal+of+Human+Movement+Science+Seeing+vs+believing&hl=en&as_sdt=0&as_vis=1&oi=scholart.

Winfrey, O. "Dnt Txt N Drv." *New York Times*. April 25, 2010. p. 13.

Wortham, J. "Angry Birds, Flocking to Cellphones Everywhere." *New York Times*. Sunday, December 12, 2010. p. 1. http://www.nytimes.com/2010/12/12/technology/12birds.html.

Zee, P. C., H. A. Emsellem, and D. Moore. "National Sleep Foundation. Sleep Report Card, 2008." http://www.sleepfoundation.org/sleep-facts-information/sleep-report-card.

Zickuhr, K. "Generations 2010." Pew Research Center. December 16, 2010. http://www.pewinternet.org/Reports/2010/Generations-2010.aspx.

About the Author

Geraldine Markel, PhD, is principal of Managing Your Mind Coaching and Seminars. She is an educational psychologist and former faculty member at the School of Education, University of Michigan. Geri has presented seminars on enhancing productivity and has written seven books focused on learning and performance. Her most recent book is, *Defeating the 8 Demons of Distractions: Proven Strategies to Increase Productivity and Decrease Stress.*

For Managing Your Mind products (including books, booklets, checklists, white papers, CDs, and digital downloads) or Managing Your Mind services (coaching and seminars), visit www.managingyourmind.com.

You can read the author's blog at http://www.demonsofdistraction.com/blog, follow her on http://twitter.com/8demons, and contact her at geri@managingyourmind. com

Index

Defeating the 8 Demons of Distraction:
Proven Strategies to Increase Productivity and Decrease Stress

This book arms workforce employees, independent professionals, and family managers with simple yet powerful strategies to defeat the 8 Demons of Distraction. Anyone who deals with stress, overcommitment, new technology, and/or special life circumstances can use these ideas to reduce common distractions and needless mistakes.

Print: $15.95 (plus S&H)

Download: $9.95

Ebook: $6.00

　　　(Available at managingyourmind.com)

Finding Your Focus:
Practical Strategies for the Everyday Challenges Facing Adults with ADD

by Judith Greenbaum, PhD, and Geraldine Markel, PhD

This easy-to-use guide provides research-based techniques to help adults manage the day-to-day problems of life with ADD at home and work. The book draws upon the authors' own experience coaching people of all ages to develop workable solutions to some of the most troubling issues they face. This book offers hands-on tips to bring order to a chaotic life; learn tactics to improve memory; improve problem-solving, decision-making, and goal-setting skills; and manage the symptoms of ADD that hinder a satisfying life.

Print and e-book available at www.Amazon.com

Personal Coaching Card Deck:
Defeating the Demons of Distraction

This deck of twenty-eight fast-reading, pocket-sized cards can be used by individuals or corporate trainers as a personal coaching tool. Each card contains a practical strategy and proverb to increase your work/life performance, decrease your stress, and improve your life.

Card Deck: $9.95 each (plus S&H)

(Significant discounts for large-quantity orders. Go to www.managingyourmind. com.)

Booklet: Defeating the Demons of Distraction:
111 Ways to Improve Work/Life Performance and Decrease Stress

A handy job aid, this 16-page 3.5 x 8.5 reference booklet shows how to combat the competing forces that can zap your focus and energy. Makes an ideal thank-you gift for clients, vendors, and friends.

Print: $5.00 (plus S&H).

Download: $4.00

　　　(Significant discounts for large quantity orders. Go to www.managingyourmind. com.)

CD: Managing Your Memory

This light, lively CD lets you discover your memory style. You'll learn to visualize items for better retention, reduce distractions that affect memory loss, and expand your memory capacity. A valuable insert helps you identify your style, keep a memory log, and use checklists, routines, and alarms.

CD: $12.95 (plus S&H)

Download: $10.00

Order Form

Qty	Title	Price	Cost
	Defeating the 8 Demons of Distraction (Book) (Download, $9.95) (Ebook, $6.00)	$15.95	
	Defeating the Demons of Distraction (Card Deck)	$9.95	
	Defeating the Demons of Distraction: 111 Ways to Improve Work/Life Performance and Decrease Stress (Booklet) (Download, $4.00)	$5.00	
	Managing Your Memory (CD) (Download, $10.00)	$12.95	
	Finding Your Focus: Practical Strategies for the Everyday Challenges Facing Adults with ADD (Book)	$16.95	
Subtotal			
Sales Tax if in MI 6%			
Shipping & Handling ($4 first book + $2 additional books)			
TOTAL			

Please enclose check/money order (check payable to Managing Your Mind, LLC). Full payment must accompany your order. Visa/MasterCard accepted for online orders only.

    Mail order and payment to:

        Managing Your Mind

        304½ South State Street

        Ann Arbor, MI 48104

        or order online at

        www.managingyourmind.com

Name _____

Address _____

City _____ State _____ Zip _____

Phone _____ E-mail _____

Downloads and large quantity discounts available at www.managingyourmind.com